Media in Situations of Conflict
Roles, Challenges and Responsibility

Editor
Adolf E. Mbaine

FOUNTAIN PUBLISHERS
Kampala

Fountain Publishers Ltd
P.O. Box 488
Kampala
Email: fountain@starcom.co.ug
Website: www:fountainpublishers.co.ug

Distributed in Europe, North America and Australia by African Books Collective
Ltd (ABC), Unit 13, Kings Meadow, Ferry Hinksey Road, Oxford OX2 0DP,
United Kingdom
Tel: 44(0) 1865-726686, Fax:44(0)1865-793298
E-mail:orders@africanbookscollective.com
abc@africanbookscollective.com
Website: www.africanbookscollective.com

© Department of Mass Communication, Makerere University 2006
First published 2006

ISBN 9970 02 536 8

Contents

Foreword   vii

Introduction   ix

1. **A Different Channel: The Role of Television in International Conflict Resolution**   1
   Michelle Betz

2. **Reporting non-stop Violence in South Africa: The Necessity for Adopting a Different Kind of Journalism**   20
   Anthea Garman

3. **The Triumph of 'Big Brother': Challenging Times for African Media in Conflict Situations**   45
   Simwogerere Kyazze

4. **The Challenges of Reporting the Northern Uganda Armed Conflict**   62
   John Muto-Ono p'Lajur

5. **Conflict in Karamoja: Bridging the Information Gap through Human Rights-Based Communication**   87
   Nathan Byamukama

6. **Media, Peace-building and the Culture of Violence**   103
   George W. Lugalambi

7. **What Role Should the Media Play in Conflict Transformation and Peace-building?**   120
   Stella M. Sabiiti

8. **Behind *The Monitor's* October 10th Shutdown**   132
   David Ouma Balikowa

9. **Partnering Civil Society with the Media in Peace-building**   139
   Deusdedit R.K. Nkurunziza

Index   153

Contributors

David Ouma Balikowa is one of the founders of the *Monitor* newspaper where he worked in various capacities as Editor until he retired from journalism in 2004. He also taught at the Department of Mass Communication, Makerere Universirty. He is now a media and communication consultant in Kampala.

Michelle Betz is a Lecturer in Radio and Television at the University of Central Florida's Nicholson School of Communication. She was awarded a Knight International Press Fellowship in 2003 and was then based at the National University of Rwanda at Butare for four months. She has also worked for the Canadian Broadcasting Corporation.

Nathan Byamukama is the head of the Department of Monitoring and Treaties at the Uganda Human Rights Commission, Kampala.

Anthea Garman is a Senior Lecturer at the Department of Journalism and Media Studies, Rhodes University, South Africa. She was a print journalist for 16 years before she became an academic. She is currently doing her PhD at the University of Witwatersrand, South Africa.

Simwogerere Kyazze is a Lecturer at the Department of Mass Communication, Makerere University. He is currently pursuing a PhD at Rhodes University in South Africa.

George William Lugalambi is a Lecturer at the Department of Mass Communication, Makerere University. He is completing his PhD at Pennyslvania State University in the United States.

John Muto-Ono p'Lajur is a journalist with the *Monitor* newspaper based in the northern Uganda town of Gulu, where he is also the Bureau Chief.

Rev. Dr Deusdedit Nkurunziza is a Senior Lecturer at the Department of Religious Studies, Makerere University. He is also the Co-ordinator of the MA Programme in Peace and Conflict Studies run by the same Department.

Stella Sabiiti is the Executive Director of the Centre for Conflict Resolution (CECORE) based in Kampala. She is also a consultant in peace-building and conflict resolution.

Foreword

Post-independent Uganda's history cannot be complete without reference to the incessant conflicts that have bedeviled this country. Armed conflict has taken permanent residence in Uganda right from the late 1970s during the liberation war that led to the ouster of the Idi Amin regime.

Then the country endured a five-year bush war from 1981 to 1986 in the former Luweero Triangle in which lives perished, property was destroyed and which led the frightened regime in Kampala into some of the worst human rights violations. In the meantime, there was another war front in West Nile and the Karamoja conflict was taking a new dimension as the Karimojong warriors also acquired sophisticated weapons, namely AK 47s.

As the Museveni-led National Resistance Army (NRA) guerillas entered Kampala City in January 1986 promising a fundamental change, one would have thought that the era of war and associated plunder belonged to the past. However, as early as August 1986, war broke out in northern Uganda and was later to spread to the Teso region in the east.

A combination of both military means and negotiation eventually brought peace to the Teso region but Karamoja and northern Uganda have remained trouble spots. In 1996, another war front opened in western Uganda as Allied Democratic Forces (ADF) attacked from the neighbouring Democratic Republic of Congo (DRC). ADF was eventually defeated in 2002.

If you add all this to the fighting that consumed Ugandan troops in the DRC from 1998 to 2003 when the Uganda People's Defence Forces (UPDF) pulled out, one can easily discern that Ugandans have for long been besieged by conflict and that every effort should be made to stop it and prevent its recurrence.

Such an effort needs the contribution of everybody: politicians, the military, civil society, academics, donors, the international community, the media, to mention but a few.

The media is especially an important player as it is ever present during any conflict and its reportage could help ease the conflict or make it worse.

The Department of Mass Communication at Makerere University, in partnership with MS Uganda, has since 1999 been trying to support the media in playing its role in constructively reporting conflict. The department has conducted training workshops in conflict reporting for rural-based journalists in northern Uganda. It has also established a Media and Peace Unit that provides information to journalists and journalism students about conflict.

Under the Media and Peace Unit, the department has also organised a public lecture series where journalists and members of the general public meet and exchange views and experiences about how best to resolve armed conflicts.

It is from these public lecture presentations, other seminar papers and solicited articles on media and peace-building that the material for this publication has been collected. The department is hopeful that this book will be found useful by media professionals and other members of the reading public in enhancing their knowledge about the media and peace.

We are grateful as a department to MS Uganda for their invaluable support towards various departmental activities and for funding the publication of the book. We are also indebted to MS Uganda for their patience as the book was supposed to be produced earlier than actually it was. The delay was due to unforeseen staff departures that necessitated internal re-organisation and re-assignment of existing staff.

We wish to express our heartfelt gratitude to Fountain Publishers for the professional job done in peer reviewing the book, editing and printing.

Finally, the authors, the editor and all who made this publication a reality are gratefully acknowledged.

We wish you good reading.

Dr G. L. Nassanga
Senior Lecturer/Head
Department of Mass Communication
Makerere University

Introduction

Even after shaking off the bondage of colonialism, nearly all the African states have had to contend with various challenges of nation-building. In several countries the march towards independence was rather involved and painful; involving bitter wars and related consequences. The scars left by the apartheid era in South Africa, whether social, political, economic or cultural before that country joined the community of civilised nations, will take a long time to heal.

But it is the challenges of putting nations together and getting the development process to start and progress that have given a stern test to the African leadership. Long after independence for most African states, the continent is still better known for all manner of crises from Luanda to Cairo and from Dar-es-Salaam to Conakry. Incessant famine, drought, floods, ebola, Aids, coups, riots, genocide and armed conflict are very consistent features of life on the African continent.

It has been argued that Africa continues to make news for all the wrong reasons because there seems to be a conspiracy by the western media to portray the continent as a lost cause, from which nothing good will come. Whereas this may be partly true, the events on the continent tend to lend credence to what appears in the international media.

For instance, the biggest catastrophe since independence in many African states has been the occurrence and re-occurrence of armed conflict in which many lives have been destroyed and a great deal of valuable property lost. States have disintegrated as a result of conflict and the development process has been arrested.

Just a few examples will illustrate this. Sudan has just come out of more that two decades of a vicious armed conflict, Liberia is holding onto some uneasy peace, while the guns have fallen silent in Sierra Leone, with no guarantee that they will not sound again. The effects of the Angolan civil war are still being assessed, after that sorry chapter in that country was closed with the death of rebel leader Jonas Savimbi in 2003. Though Mozambique has perhaps completely resolved all the internal contradictions that led to that devastating civil war of the eighties, its legacy will remain for many generations.

Closer home, the impact of the Rwanda genocide in 1994 that shook the entire world is still reverberating. One wonders why people from the same country would seize every available opportunity to descend on one another with such a hot and sordid passion. Burundi has just made some strides towards democratisation and peace, after a well-calculated intervention both at regional and continental levels.

On the home front Karamoja conflict seems to be on the rise and will, unless resolved now, be beyond redemption. The proliferation of arms in the region has made the Karamoja security problem intractable, and the immediate consequences of this have been massacres, cattle rustling and property destruction, driving people in the neighbouring areas of Teso, especially, into camps.

The Karamoja problem will also persist mainly because of its international dimension but also because the Ugandan national army has been consumed by civil war in northern Uganda for the last 19 years, and the end of this war seems nowhere in sight. Both the military means and peace talks have failed to save the region from the marauding Lord's Resistance Army (LRA) led by the reclusive Joseph Kony who for long was known to be fighting to establish a government based on the biblical Ten Commandments.

Even with a semblance of peace in Sudan in the aftermath of the peace agreement signed on January 2005 (whose future hung in the balance following the death of former rebel leader and Sudan's First Vice President John Garang at the end of July 2005), the LRA continues to operate mainly in southern Sudan from where they frequently return to visit mayhem on the people of northern Uganda.

Uganda has also had to deal with the Allied Democratic Forces (ADF) rebellion that started in 1996 but was brought to an end in 2002, although there are reported ADF remnants in the Democratic Republic of Congo (DRC). Of course Uganda was one of the foreign forces that occupied most of eastern DRC from 1998 to 2003 where it fought several armies including that of its former ally, Rwanda.

Therefore, a number of African countries, including Uganda, have been at the receiving end of conflict and it behoves everyone who can make a contribution to play a role. Conflicts are devastating and too complicated to be left only to the combatants and a few peace-makers to resolve. Stemming conflict would now seem to require the contribution of everyone: governments, politicians, civic and religious leaders, the military, community-based and civil society organisations, donors, the mass media, to mention but a few.

The media in particular has been brought into sharp focus recently as a key player in conflict whose role needs to be revisited. War necessarily makes news, as conflict is a time-tested news value. It has also been the view held by many that the level and orientation of coverage of a war by the mass media may easily escalate or reduce it. It has thus become imperative for the media, especially in Africa, to understand conflict and appreciate its role in covering it so that war reports are done consciously and effectively.

It would also be worthwhile for African journalists to adopt a different king of journalism as advanced by Anthea Garman in this book. The media has a responsibility to make ordinary citizens feel safe and secure so that they can meaningfully participate in the demo-cratic and development process.

Adolf E. Mbaine
Editor

1

A Different Channel:
The Role of Television in International
Conflict Resolution

Michelle Betz

Since World War II, the extensive use of the mass media in diplomacy,
the so-called "public diplomacy", has transformed both the appearance
and the substance of diplomacy (Van Dinh, 1988, p.37).

Tran Van Dinh, in his book *Communication and Diplomacy in a Changing
World*, suggests that the mass media have helped transform diplomacy
today, but this researcher would suggest that the most influential and
important medium shaping diplomacy today is television. This paper will
examine the new roles or uses of the media, in particular, the role television
plays in international conflict resolution and diplomacy. It will also discuss
how technological changes coupled with continuing transformations in
the international arena may ultimately bring about new or alternative roles
for television in international conflict. This will be examined particularly
vis-à-vis that part of the conflict known as resolution.

The analysis of the new roles or uses of the media is relevant for several
reasons. First, it may alter traditional methods and standards of journalism
and/or roles of journalists. Second, conflict resolution continues to hold
importance in international affairs as long as there are outbreaks of war.
Thus, if we consider television an important, and perhaps *the* most
important and influential, medium of communication it must, in some
ways, be intrinsic to conflict resolution.

Rarely has there been an examination of the media outside the traditional
role of news gatherers and disseminators. In doing precisely this, however,
it becomes clear that there exist other relations between military and media
besides the traditional antagonism and that these two bodies may, in fact,
be able to work together in bringing about positive ends to a conflict.

1

What does it mean, for example, to be an information conduit? What possible roles exist for the media and individual journalists in conflict resolution, and should they be playing such roles? Will technological developments force changes on the role of the media in future relations with the military, particularly during times of international conflict, or is this too already taking place? How has technology affected the ideal of objectivity and the role of the journalist? Are media becoming more partisan owing to external circumstances? And, finally, in light of these questions, should journalistic standards be altered? These are some of the questions this paper will address.

Finally, this paper offers a number of guidelines for how the journalistic, diplomatic and military communities might deal with tele-diplomacy, or diplomacy by way of television.

Diplomacy and Tele-Diplomacy

One of the most elementary definitions of diplomacy is provided by Briggs (1968):

> Diplomacy is the conduct on official business by trained personnel representing governments. The purpose of diplomacy is to reach agreement within a framework of policy (p.202).

It is important to note the reference to trained personnel in this definition. What implications could this have for journalists who are not trained in the field of diplomacy? What implications could it have for diplomats? And what precisely is involved in a diplomat's work? The major activities of the diplomat can be divided into three categories: negotiation, representation, and reporting. It is this last activity of reporting which is of particular relevance here for it is this in which journalists are engaged as well.

The broadcast media fulfil not only the traditional role of reporting the news. They also are often able to cut through bureaucracy; in doing so they can reach government leaders, affect official priorities, help set policy and mobilise public opinion (Davison, 1974, p.6). Michael Gurevitch (1991) too has noted the potential influence of television in such circumstances. He suggests that television can act as a "go-between, a channel of communication especially in instances in which hostile relationships between governments tend to preclude direct contacts" (p.187).

This research would suggest that television not only has the potential to operate, but perhaps already does so, as a quasi-diplomat; a phenomenon called tele-diplomacy. This type of diplomacy readily bypasses diplomatic channels with television acting as an alternative source of information for diplomats when regular channels may be closed. It is also important to bear in mind that one crucial element of conflict resolution is diplomacy. O'Heffernan (1991) suggests that television not only functions in foreign policy as a rapid source of information useful for policy decisions, but is also a "proxy for diplomats" as well as a "diplomatic signalling system with policy influence" (p.37). O'Heffernan also suggests that television has the ability to set policy agendas. Perhaps the biggest problem with this, as alluded to above, is that policies are carried out without much thought; long-term policies are likely to be sacrificed for short-term palliatives.

Moreover, because television is preoccupied with visual images, it is seldom as reflective or as organised as print. Government leaders consequently have come to rely on pictures and emotions rather than argument. Thoughts are expressed in sound bites and rational discourse is avoided. Information is moved, but rarely explained or analysed. As Webster (1990) says: "This national problem becomes more severe in the international cross-cultural Babel of misunderstanding" (p.120).

At one time observers thought that the development of new technologies would make television more thorough and complete in its coverage, but the most recent breakthroughs – small video cameras, satellites and videophones – have actually been a setback to the quality of coverage:

> Because it is now possible to fly a crew to the scene of a crisis and instantaneously send back information, television is even more addicted to "parachute" journalism than before...Correspondents now seem to spend more time jet-setting than concentrating on a small handful of countries. Moreover, reporting in one time zone while feeding stories to New York on another can make for gruelling eighteen-hour days, hardly a lifestyle conducive to reflective reporting (Gergen, 1990, p.51).

As a result, there are still many who turn to print for analysis of what is shown on television.

Davison (1974) explains how the media may influence policy:

> [The media] help to set an agenda for political leaders, as they do for the general public; they provide these leaders with much of the

information on which decisions are based; they likewise influence the experts and "elites" who in turn influence the decision-makers; they affect public opinion on specific issues and the public mood in general, thus limiting of expanding the alternatives that political leaders can realistically consider; and they provide channels through which governments must explain their policies in order to obtain the consent or co-operation of the governed (p.15).

Clearly, an intimate relationship exists between communication and diplomacy, which is essentially an act of communication. But one must then ask what the route of this communication is. If there exists the possibility that television may be taking on a new role, what implications exist for the journalist who may, *de facto*, be acting in the capacity of the diplomat? How has the globalisation of television news extended to the field of diplomacy and on to the relatively new phenomenon of tele-diplomacy?

Tele-diplomacy has the potential to be extremely useful during conflict resolution situations and there seems to be an increasing tendency for the media to become a part of the intergovernmental and diplomatic process with the media often acting as the communication channel between governments and publics.

The CNN Factor

Canadian Major-General Lewis Mackenzie (retd) (personal communication, November 1993) believes there is a very important role to be played by the media that the military ignores at its peril. It is too early to discern whether or not this process is effective; however, implications abound and not solely for the media's role in this business, but also on diplomatic and military levels. Government leaders increasingly rely on the likes of CNN, and more recently al-Jazeera, to garner information on world events. Public reportage has become a factor in decision-making as extensive and instantaneous coverage itself becomes part of the decision environment for a variety of interests and audiences. This is a radical change from the past when the role of the news media was simply to report the news rather than to act as a conduit or, to some extent, act as a participant.

In the past, events that became crises typically began outside the purview of all but a few and were allowed to develop without great concern for public opinion. Today, such concealment is virtually impossible. Media outlets facilitate the exchange of views among conflicting parties. If government leaders formulate their strategies to appeal to the public who are generally interested in peaceful resolutions, this could have the effect of conditioning the formulation and execution of foreign policy with the possibility of moderating conflicts and heading off crises before they mature (Davison, 1974, p.6).

This illustrates the profound impact the broadcast media may have on various phases of international affairs and policy-making. Not only are the media used to facilitate the exchange of views but they are also useful for communicating government messages to the public. Images gained from television can also be beneficial for military purposes. One such example was during the 1991 Gulf War. According to a Canadian military official (personal communication, 1994) the Iraqis did not provide the rest of the world with weather forecasts for Iraq thus creating problems for the allied forces as military officials could not make adjustments on target selection without weather information. But the CNN reports out of Baghdad solved this problem: "They [the allied forces] were watching CNN to see what the weather conditions were in downtown Baghdad because they were the most accurate and timely source of weather information and the only source." By watching these reports, the allies could make any necessary adjustments before going out on bombing runs leading to an "unintentional use of a media product" (Wills, 1994).

Ultimately, the role of the journalist extends beyond that of the traditional witness. Instead, it seems the media have become participants in world events. Gurevitch (1991), for example, describes how television has become an integral part of day-to-day events:

> The enhancement of the roles, and the powers, of television can be traced to its emergence, in the era of instant global communication, as an *active participant in the events it purportedly "covers"*. Television can no longer be regarded (if it ever was) as a mere observer and reporter of events. It is inextricably locked into these events, and has clearly become an integral part of the reality it reports. The notion that television, and the media generally, should be more properly regarded as participants in the world they report on, rather than observers has for many years, and still is, a controversial one. For it challenges one of the central tenets of Western journalism, namely that the media should stand "outside", and be detached from, the subjects of their reporting, if they are to be true to the norms of objectivity, impartiality and neutrality (Gurevitch, 1991, p.185).

But what are the implications of such participation? Is it possible for the media to maintain a clear distinction between covering an event and participating in it? This researcher would suggest that it is this last distinction that becomes crucial in the discussion of tele-diplomacy and the role of the journalist in situations such as those described. This is crucial because we must then discern if or how a journalist might be useful without jeopardising his/her standards of professional objectivity and without threatening a peace that may hang in a delicate balance. But there are also problems attached to this type of policy-making.

Challenges Involving the Role of Television in Conflict Resolution

Over-Reliance on Television as an Information Source
Some who have been directly involved with television in diplomacy or conflict resolution find the prospect of a continued, and perhaps increasing, role for television quite frightening. General Mackenzie, for example, believes that technological advancements have changed diplomacy, decision-making and foreign policy objectives because of an apparently diminishing use of other information outlets. The difficulty, he says, lies in the significance attached to television that in some cases outweighs other considerations, such as government briefings which usually take a long time to circulate. Mackenzie gives the example of Somalia: "We put all this effort into Somalia and twice as many people were dying in the Sudan from natural famine and not civil war-induced famine. Equal numbers were also dying in Liberia, Angola and Mozambique but there were no cameras there" (personal communication). Indeed, the presence of cameras in Somalia and manipulation by the warring parties ultimately forced the US contingent to pull out of the United Nations operation in that country.

Mackenzie also sees an over-reliance by policy-makers on television as a source of information:

> Within democracies where elected people respond to their electorate, where the electorate takes its impressions from television and then passes them on to their elected representatives, the elected representatives react to that when in fact they should be reacting to a whole bunch of other things like...satellite imagery and diplomatic corps, military attaches, military intelligence. All of those things should

be put together in a hopper and evaluated and then priorities assigned (Personal communication, 1993).

Mackenzie admits the medium should in no way be dismissed, but he advises a degree of caution by government and military officials.

Television Increases the Number of Players

First, the number of players increases because of television; in fact, television, and thus the broadcast media, is one of these players. If this is the case, then one must also consider the role that self-interest plays in such circumstances. As O'Heffernan (1991) explains, "The media are independent entities functioning to meet their individual self-interests...Media organisations share the limitations and advantages of their technology, the incentive structures of ratings and profits, and the cultural dimensions of journalistic ethics and comradeship" (p.86).

Self-Interest

> At a business level, the different outlets are increasingly competing for each other's audiences and advertisers, injecting a strong reporting incentive to get the story first, but an equally strong incentive to get the story that will grab their audience and allow them to attract viewers or readers from the competition (O'Heffernan p.87).

However, there exists a paradox in this element of self-interest. While O'Heffernan suggests the media are independent entities, a different type of self-interest, which cannot be ignored, is manifested particularly during conflicts – patriotism and national interest. Although the media's sphere of operation and coverage has become global, worldviews are still fairly parochial.

The 1991 Gulf War is a good illustration of this loyalty. Many journalists felt they were relegated to the role of patriotic cheerleaders in that their coverage was severely limited and, in fact, consisted largely of ready-made press releases or daily briefings with little, if any, access to the field. While this may not have been by choice, the fact remains that there was little, if any, critical or investigative coverage on the part of Western journalists during that war. While there were some attempts to change this during the recent Gulf War, for example the allies' practice of embedding journalists with troops, there was still little critical journalism, particularly on the part of American journalists.

Some believe that this lack of critical voices during the first weeks of the 1991 war exposes the "timidity, narrowness and fundamental subservience of the mainstream media, especially the television networks, in the United States. The broadcast media are afraid to go against a perceived popular consensus, to alienate people, or to take unpopular stands because they are afraid of losing viewers and thus profits" (Kellner, 1991, p.85 and Wolff, personal communication, 1994). Yet another writer, Dan Hallin (1986), in writing about the Vietnam War, said:

> Those reporters also went to Southeast Asia schooled in a set of journalistic practices which, among other things, ensures that the news would reflect, if not always the views of those at the very top of the American political hierarchy, at least the perspective of American officialdom generally…[And] the reporters also went to Vietnam deeply committed to the "national security" consensus that had dominated American politics since the onset of the Cold War, and acted as "responsible" advocates of that consensus (Hallin, pp.8-9).

Television as a Propaganda Tool

The media usually side with the perceived national interests of the system of which they are a part. This, of course, makes it difficult to maintain journalistic independence and neutrality in the face of patriotism and national loyalty. Mowlana (1985) recognises this tension between professional norms and patriotism. "One function of diplomacy – representation – contradicts the traditional spirit of 'objectivity' inherent in the classical role of a journalist; to represent one view over another is to forsake a position of neutrality. It implies the use (voluntary or otherwise) of the media as a tool to be manipulated" (in Arno, p.86). Underlying the question of self-interest seems to be an unavoidable conflict in the duty of the journalist: to learn and report what he/she can about a story, and not be used as a propaganda tool.

One of the clearest examples of this was during the 1991 Gulf War. Peter Arnett, a CNN correspondent who stayed in Baghdad once the bombing began, was accused, often unfairly, of being a traitor. George Wolff (personal communication, 1994), a Canadian foreign correspondent, believes that the kind of questioning that was raised of Arnett's patriotism and about the value of what he was doing was unfair:

> What he was doing was very valuable; it just wasn't in line with official doctrine. There's tremendous pressure, not just from the media but

from home, to take the patriotic line and I know that was the case...More power to him for his guys and what he said. It was critical of the kind of patriotic rhetoric that became so popular during the war where Saddam Hussein and the whole Iraqi side became vilified without any kind of understanding; they just became the enemy...That's the one thing to watch out for in these situations, is the patriotic sentiment which even reporters feel. We've got to be with our side.

It is this inherent conflict or paradox which becomes evident during times of conflict in particular, and it raises questions as to whether journalistic standards should be altered. While this is perhaps a larger question and is to a great extent beyond the scope of this paper, it is one that, with it, brings implications for journalists, in particular regarding ethical issues. Should the journalistic community have condemned Arnett, for example? Clearly, reporting from behind Iraqi lines served a useful journalistic purpose. For some time he was the only Western reporter working out of Baghdad, but because he did this CNN was regarded by many as unethical and unpatriotic. Despite this, it was probably better to have a Western reporter behind the lines than to have all the news coming from Iraqi sources.

According to one Canadian Department of National Defence spokesperson, however, when television acts as an intermediary the overwhelming interest will always be profit. This raises the question of which will take precedence – bias/national self-interest or profit? In the Arnett case, bias was the overruling factor and, coupled with traditional news values, pushed CNN to allow Arnett to stay in Baghdad to file his stories.

While there may be those who suggest that the internationalisation of the media means national identities will play a less and less important role, it is not clear whether this will be the case simply because those "internationalised" journalists for the most part still file to countries with similar political systems, values and ideals. CNN, for example, still has a distinctly American bias despite being an international service.

Television Affects the Pace of Foreign Policy

O'Heffernan (1991) also suggested that television affects foreign policy (and thus, this researcher would add, conflict resolution) by accelerating the pace of that same policy. O'Heffernan describes this as the "fast-forward" effect. There is an important element of time inherent in tele-diplomacy. Satellite and videophone technology allows journalists not only to overcome the power of the military and government to control the flow of information, but allows them to escape the element of time. Real-time images and reports require governments to catch up, and they can force officials to make quick decisions without thoroughly examining options. As Kellner (1992) suggests, this places undue strain on a system which is, more often than not, already overloaded. "Governments need time to react and believe they should not be pressurised by the media into making premature and potentially dangerous decisions" (Kellner, p.43).

Real-time images can create a false illusion of immediate authenticity, creating problems for both reporters and officials. The reporter's ability to assess critically what is happening is reduced, as is the possibility of maintaining a balanced distance from events. This can lead to a chain of events which, if not carefully watched, may create "an incestuous cycle of misinformation with one news organisation feeding off another: a print newsroom may feed off the television news channel, and the television news channel may 'harden' its own coverage under the influence of a dubious newspaper story" (Hopkinson, 1992, p.35).

Major Wills, for example, said that "when time is of the essence, senior [military] management may be tempted to make an ill-informed decision based on what they just saw on CNN" (personal communication). A situation may be projected as more volatile than it really is, causing a response that is not as well thought out as it could be. Basically, there simply is not time (or at least it is thought not to exist) to make a well-informed decision. Instant technology has also created high viewer expectations which, coupled with the capital tied up in technology on location, puts pressure on journalists to have content ready when in fact there may be no story to report:

> The result can be a rambling string of inaccuracies which misinform or cause even greater problems. Thus diplomats frequently complain that their staffs have to waste time verifying whether television reports are accurate, rectifying the errors and repairing the diplomatic damage. Governments and politicians need time to respond and make up their own minds, rather than have their decisions determined prematurely by the media (Hopkinson, 1992, p.35).

While it is not clear to what extent this may happen, the simple fact that it could create potential logistical nightmares for diplomats cannot be ignored.

One example of this type of problem was illustrated during the 1991 Gulf War. While television acted mostly as a communicator during that war, there were also times when the medium acted more like a policy-maker thereby creating some problems. Hopkinson (1992) explains:

> Portable satellite facilities enabled journalists to transmit independently of government and military control, and the military and governments no longer controlled the flow of information. Images were relayed to the public well before diplomats or the military could communicate the situation to decision-makers. Governments had to catch up with public opinion, and sometimes were pressurised into making rapid, even premature decisions. For example, during the first hours of the SCUD attacks on Israel some US television networks mistakenly alleged or implied that the missiles were carrying chemical weapons. These panic-stricken live broadcasts almost forced the Israeli government to ignore the intense diplomatic pressure being applied by President Bush, Under-Secretary of State Eagleburger, and others to keep Israel out of the war (p.29).

It is potential diplomatic and military disasters such as this which, if tele-diplomacy is to gain momentum, must be avoided.

The sheer speed of the technology today leaves no time for reflection or interpretation and despite problems such as those above, diplomats still rely on the broadcast media as one of their main sources of information precisely because of the speed. While diplomats have long garnered information from the media, the speed of the technology alters the media's role. O'Heffernan (1991) describes what the consequences of this might be:

> Mass media may reduce central command and control over police in some circumstances involving embassy staff. The immediate delivery of issue-sensitive information to embassies and consulates and to the people and the leadership of host nations pose an interesting problem for the consular staff. They must decide whether to withhold response to media inquiries locally before getting guidance from Washington [or the country capital], and be called indecisive, or to respond without knowing what policy response is being developed in their capital (which received the same news but may move slower because of a larger bureaucracy), and risk embarrassing their government (p.95).

The former Vietnamese Ambassador to France has noted that the speed of diplomatic messages in the last century went from weeks to minutes. Clearly that has now changed to seconds. Van Dinh (1988) suggests this puts pressure on governments to act because of the problem has become public information and constituencies want to know what is being done. Television therefore has the ability to force deadlines that the policy process on its own might not have set (O'Heffernan, 1991, p.101).

Other Problems

Other challenges exist as well. If one country's officials rely on the media for information then officials of another government may very well have incentive to use the news to transmit information to them. Continued long enough, this could lead to the use of the media for disinformation or for dissemination of material that is relevant, but misleading or untrue. Inevitably, "information in the news aimed at the home front gets entangled in international politics just as information targeted for foreign officials becomes accessible to domestic audiences in various capitals" (Sigal, 1973, p.151).

There are other problems inherent in the medium of television itself, such as heavy reliance on visual images. What happens when a story is led by pictures? Neil Postman (1985), for example, believes that pictures "have no difficulty overwhelming words and short-circuiting introspection" (p.103). Indeed, pictures are inevitably emphasised over words and those stories that are not visual are often omitted altogether or at least shortened and simplified. Lack of analysis ensues and the image dominates over words and explanation.

On the other hand, strong emotional television pictures might be so dramatic as to make political pressure to do something irresistible. This pressure is often articulated in the op-ed pages of newspapers where the recommendations of policy-makers have been sharpened by the pictures shown on previous days. But, in many cases, television is better at conveying emotion rather than factual information.

Television could hinder foreign policy-making and diplomacy in other ways. For example, by interacting with other parties and simply being involved in the process of tele-diplomacy, the medium could very well reduce central control over diplomatic and political activities, reduce the amount of secrecy in diplomatic affairs, and provide amounts of information to policy officials and diplomats worldwide that are beyond their capability to assimilate and verify (O'Heffernan p.79). Indeed, as one writer puts it:

We are experiencing today only the initial impact of the new forms of international electronic distribution and the creation of "populist diplomacy". National leaders, more and more, appeal directly to constituencies in other nations. This international political discourse, often including players unauthorised by officialdom, exists alongside traditional controlled intergovernmental transactions (Webster, 1990, p.219).

Conclusion

Ultimately, it appears the role of broadcast journalism is changing regarding foreign affairs in part owing to external circumstances. Indeed, this researcher suggested at the outset of this paper that technological and global developments have or will force changes on the role of the media in future relations with both governments and militaries.

As suggested in this paper, over-reliance on the television news media, self-interest of individual journalists, television news and its journalists can be considered players on the global scene resulting in an increase in the total number of players. These factors, together with the use of television as a propaganda tool, are all forcing a change in the way television and journalists operate and are used in international conflict situations, in particular when it comes to resolving conflict.

These changes have brought the idea (or perhaps the ideal) of objectivity into question. The French sociologist Jacques Ellul (1973) believed that propaganda is an inevitable political response to the communications revolution "which pervades all aspects of life" (p. xvii). If, indeed, this is the case, then how has technology affected this ideal of objectivity and the role of the journalist today? Are the media becoming more partisan owing to external circumstances as they were in the 19th century?

This researcher believes the answer to the latter is a definitive yes. This may be disturbing for media practitioners and those who uphold the ideal of objectivity, claiming that the raison d'etre of journalism is this ideal. And there are those who suggest that, in the context of this paper, the media could become involved in conflict management structures only if certain conditions prevail. These include a "stance of disinterest", or perhaps more appropriately, objectivity, and "a high level of integrity" (Arno, 1984, p.236).

Indeed, this paper has emphasised the positive aspects of television's role in international conflict and its resolution, and thus, has presupposed objectivity. It has been suggested, for example, that television can: increase the quantity of information and international communication; increase the quality; provide early warning of situations which might lead to conflict; make policy-makers aware of potential opportunities which might help to increase international understanding; stimulate the use of mechanisms of conflict resolution whether negotiations, mediation and arbitration and provide information that might facilitate these processes; help to create a mood in which peaceful solutions are more likely to be sought and accepted (see Davison, 1974). In order to do most of these things, however, the media must be truly objective or at the very least on all sides to the best of their abilities, something which is often difficult at the best of times and quite possibly impossible during times of conflict, thus barring potential positive roles in resolution of these same conflicts.

One author has written that "blinded by their adherence to the false concept of 'objectivity', the media perceive themselves as somehow operating outside society, eschewing all responsibility for what takes place within it (Mowlana in Arno, 1984, p.71). Indeed, it is precisely views such as this that must change, or perhaps are already changing.

It is equally important to recognise that television and television news can be a double-edged sword: on one hand exists the danger of propaganda, while on the other is the ideal of objectivity. Given this, what is the purpose of television in conflict resolution? If the media are to be objective then how can they possibly become involved in conflict management? This seems to present a fundamental contradiction as it goes against traditional journalistic values of non-partisanship. But it is precisely owing to this contradiction that, this researcher would suggest, the media are experiencing changes in their role and also in the way that role is perceived by other actors on the international scene.

There does exist, this researcher would suggest, an opportunity for the broadcast media to play an important and perhaps decisive role in conflict resolution. This researcher would further suggest that this role is often completely out of the hands of the media practitioners themselves; instead, a multitude of other actors use the media to their own ends. While this is not an entirely new phenomenon, it does bring into question the true independence of the media.

It also calls into question what precisely the role of television news is on the global scene. There is perhaps no definitive answer to this particular question. However, if nothing else, this paper has sought to examine the elements involved in the continuing evolution of this medium, and, if not providing definitive answers, at least it might serve to further our understanding of the variety of interactions and the true complexities of the situation at hand.

Clearly, just as there are innumerable factors at play during a conflict situation, so too are there when trying to resolve a conflict. Television is the only actor among a multitude of changing actors and it can only be understood with a consideration of all the elements at play in such situations.

Television news, like the newspaper before it, is experiencing changes. In the words of Robert E. Park (Roshco, 1975):

> The newspaper, like the modern city, is not a wholly rational product. No one sought to make it just what it is. In spite of all the efforts of individual men and generations of men to control it and to make it something after their own heart, it has continued to grow and change in its own incalculable ways (p.24).

Indeed, this researcher would suggest that television news is evolving in a similar fashion often with little opportunity for journalists to control the way in which it is used.

George Wolff, Canadian Television's former London bureau chief, believes the media can be both beneficial and harmful to resolution processes. He believes that relentless European coverage finally forced action in the former Yugoslavia:

> I don't think the Bosnia peace would have happened if television wasn't in there showing the bombing of the market and the bodies being dragged out. The world finally got so shocked it said "enough, enough, we'll bomb the hell out of the people who are laying siege to the city" (personal communication, 1994).

Wolff's suggestion of simply letting the broadcast media "do their job", and the presumption that such independence is possible, may be idealistic. There have always been, and there will continue to be, outside factors which influence the process of journalism, whether systemic economic, military or government pressure. Government and military officials alike have become much more adept and sophisticated at using television as a means of diplomacy. However, one cannot ignore that the greatest potential contributions of television and tele-diplomacy to peaceful conflict resolution lie in the media's ability to influence the moods of government, elites, and the public.

Guidelines

This final section is intended to provide some basic guidelines and suggestions to the parties involved – the media, government and military – to help them adapt to this period of change. Many of these suggestions are based simply on increased awareness of changing roles within the global community, advancing technology, and educating those who often have to work together amidst these changes.

Finally, despite past antagonisms between the parties involved, it appears the only way to move forward productively in a world experiencing continuing changes is to have increasing co-operation among global actors. If television can mobilise for war and exacerbate tensions then surely the medium should be able to do the reverse and play a role in resolving conflicts.

1. Government and military officials should learn about the requirements and expectations of foreign news agencies. They could therefore understand how reporting can exert a major influence on the course of world events. They should understand the operational and technological constraints under which the media work.

2. Global news operations, such as CNN, and the journalists working for them, should recognise the impact of their broadcasts not just on military security but also on diplomatic relations. This might then create further awareness of their immense responsibility.

3. Those working in broadcasting, particularly where communications can be transmitted instantaneously, should be more aware of the media's ability to influence events during, preceding, or following a period of tension. There also exist dangers of manipulation and disinformation.

4. Those involved in the types of situations discussed should be aware of all the elements involved in the various processes. It is important to understand the actors involved and what role each plays.

5. Journalists must understand the inherent power and authority given to the medium of television. They should further recognise that it often overrides people's own ideas of a particular situation. They should also be aware of their role as third parties. Because television provides an effective forum for information and communication, there will always be those who will try to control news content in an effort to affect the outcome of war and diplomatic efforts. Journalists must be

aware of the phenomenal consequences their reports may produce despite pressures of accuracy, deadlines, objectivity, and even patriotism.

6. Education about the role of the media in peace and war times should be part of military training at all levels. This should include education about new technologies and their effects both on how the media operate and how they might affect military and diplomatic operations.

7. Journalism education should include tutoring in the role of the media in international affairs. In light of continuing technological advances, the broadcast media in particular should be focused on.

8. Efforts should be made to have joint seminars or training sessions involving representatives from the military, government and the media so that all can at least work with a basic knowledge of how the others operate. Their relationships would then be founded on experience rather than hearsay.

9. Media participation in military exercises and military training courses should be encouraged to help increase awareness of mutual problems among the military and the media.

10. The government and military must accept that the continuing growth of communications technology will make it increasingly difficult for one country to maintain control over the flow of information.

11. The government and/or military could organise a working committee to monitor developments in communications technology and likely implications. This could be done in conjunction with broadcasters.

12. The military should recognise that the impact of new communications technology increases the need to develop better relations with the media in order to increase trust.

13. The media can increase the amount of information available on peaceful solutions to conflict. This information might simply include breaking down stereotypes and reminding parties involved of peaceful solutions.

14. Government and military officials should refrain from making decisions based on information garnered from only one source, particularly if that source is "real-time" television news. Policy-makers should address this dilemma and not be pressured into making premature decisions.

References

Arno, A. & Dissanayake, W. (Eds.). (1984). *The News Media in National and International Conflict.* Boulder: Westview Press, Inc.

Briggs, E. (1968). *Anatomy of Diplomacy: The Origin and Execution of American Foreign Policy.* New York: David McKay.

Davison, W.P. (1974). *Mass Communication and Conflict Resolution.* New York: Praeger.

Ellul, J. (1973). *Propaganda: The Formation of Men's Attitudes.* New York: Vintage Books.

Gergen, D.R. (1990) Diplomacy in a Television Age. In Serfaty, S. (Ed.) *The Media and Foreign Policy.* New York: St. Martin's Press.

Graef, R. (1993 September 22). "Negotiations, Peace and Journalists". *The London Times.*

Gurevitch, M. (1991). The Globalization of Electronic Media. In Curran, J. and Gurevitch, M. (Eds.) *Mass Media and Society.* New York: Routledge, Chapman and Hall.

Hallin, D.C. (1986). *The "Uncensored War": The Media and Vietnam.* New York: Oxford University Press.

Hopkinson, N. (1992 June). *War and the Media. Wilton Park Paper 55.* London: HMSO.

Kellner, D. (1992) *The Persian Gulf TV War.* Boulder: Westview Press, Inc.

LaMay, C., FitzSimon, M. & Sahadieds, J. (1991) *The Media at War: The Press and the Persian Gulf Conflict.* New York: Gannett Foundation.

MacKenzie, Major-General L. (ret'd). (1993 November). Personal interview.

Mowlana, H., Gerbner, G. & Schiller, H.I. (Eds.) (1992). *Triumph of the Image: The Media's War in the Persian Gulf – A Global Perspective.* Boulder: Westview Press, Inc.

O'Heffernan, P. (1991). *Mass Media and American Foreign Policy.* New Jersey: Ablex Publishing Co.

Postman, N. (1985). *Amusing Ourselves to Death*. New York: Penguin Books.

Roshco, B. (1975). *Newsmaking*. Chicago: Chicago University Press.

Sigal, L. (1973). *Reporters and Officials: The Organization and Politics of Newsmaking*. Lexington, MA: D.C. Heath.

Turner, G. (1993 July 4). "The World in a Box". *The London Telegraph*.

Van Dinh, T. (1988). *Communication and Diplomacy in a Changing World*. New Jersey: Ablex Publishing Co.

Webster, D. (1990). "New Communications Technology and the International Political Process". In Serfaty, S. (Ed.). *The Media and Foreign Policy*. New York: St. Martin's Press.

Wills, Major S. Department of National Defence (Canada) Public Affairs. (1994 January). Personal interview.

Wolff, G. Former Canadian Television (CTV) News London Bureau Chief. (1994 February). Personal interview.

Young, C. (1991). *The Role of the Media in International Conflict. CIIPS Working Paper 38*. Canadian Institute of International Peace and Security.

2

Reporting non-stop Violence in South Africa: The Necessity for Adopting a Different Kind of Journalism

Anthea Garman

South Africa is not at war, and is very unlikely to go to war, any time soon. When the government wants to spend R40 billion on new machines of war, the citizenry is horrified, so distant seems the need to protect our national borders from invasion. As a new nation in the world community, we have willingly relinquished our ability to make nuclear weapons. We have recently prosecuted (although not successfully) one of the architects of our own chemical weapons programme. The newest occupation we put our defence force to is joining international peace-keeping forces, and we bask in national pride about the transition of our military from a feared and hated force in the sub-region into a spearhead for peace in the rest of Africa. We have one of the most enlightened constitutions in the world, one which unusually enshrines women's rights and outlaws racism and homophobia. We uphold freedom of expression, the independence of the judiciary and the rule of Parliament. And yet, South Africa is not a safe place to live. Violence is everywhere, on the streets, in the homes. The public debate about "ordinary violence" has been growing steadily since the democratic transition of 1994 with perceptions, fuelled by news media reports, that the incidence of criminality has been on the rise since the end of apartheid.

Since 1994 the private security industry has burgeoned to keep middle-class citizens safe from the criminals the police force cannot protect them against. Violence manifests itself in this "transformed" society in:

- Appalling rape statistics (1.6 million women and children were raped or sexually assaulted in 1999 according to the MTN Crime Prevention Centre at Rhodes University[1]).

- Widespread abuse of children (physical, sexual and abandonment to the streets of the cities[2]).

- Terrible numbers of those murdered (in 1998, 59 per 100 000 population murders took place – this compared to 56 in Colombia and 9 in Zimbabwe[3]).

- Hijacks and a booming industry in stolen cars and car parts (74 000 cars were reported stolen in 2001[4]).

- Robberies with a dangerous weapon and involving serious injury – an increase of 25 000 a year from 1994 to 2001.[5]

- Farm murders and massacres still taking place in rural areas.[6]

- Drug-related gang wars and anti-gang vigilantism.[7]

- Taxi wars – in 1998, 291 people died in this kind of aggression.[8]

- Hostility and irrational violence against African migrants who come to South Africa with hope, but soon find themselves on the receiving end of attacks because they look and act differently.[9]

- Random and bizarre attacks on individuals seen to be a threat to communities – such as the killing of Gugu Dlamini who revealed her HIV-positive status through the media on World Aids Day in 1998.[10]

- The persecution and torture of those thought to be witches or to deal in body parts.[11]

- A society awash in guns – "Nobody really knows how many illegal firearms there are in South Africa, with estimates ranging between 500 000 and 4 million," says the Gun Control Alliance. The GCA also reports that 60 legal guns are reported stolen a day.[12]

- The Institute for Security Studies (ISS) also points out that of the 2 575 617 crimes recorded in 2000, 24% got to court (609 928), 11% were brought to trial (271 057), resulting in 211 762 convictions (8% of the total).[13]

- A post-1994 wave of emigration of mostly white South Africans for whom increasing crime is the major reason for leaving the country.[14]

In an assessment of the SA Police Services statistics for 2002 (the latest available), ISS researcher, Sibusiso Masuku, says: "The high volume of violent crimes, in particular interpersonal violent crime, is worrying. The

SAPS has classified most of these crimes as social fabric crimes, to highlight the little control police have over these crimes... strategies aimed at reducing these crimes are heavily dependant on serious investment in the social and economic development of the country's poor."[15]

So if there is not officially a 'conflict' taking place, how are we to understand the level, range and variety of devastatingly violent practices going on in South Africa at the moment?[16]

Another critical question to be asked by those of us involved in media work is about the reporting of this variety of violence. Since the demise of the apartheid regime and the shift to 'normality', many South African newsrooms have returned to beat reporting that relegates violence of any sort to the pigeonholes of crime and courts. In the 1980s during the states of emergency, my experience in the *Natal Witness* newsroom in Pietermaritzburg (which found itself at the heart of the ANC/Inkatha Freedom Party civil war) was that specialist reporters, who were more akin to investigative journalists, handled the reporting of violence. This may not have been a deliberate strategy, but the danger (both physical and political) in working in this territory was so high, that those who proved themselves particularly adept at making contacts, figuring out the intricacies and staying alive to bring back the stories, created a niche for themselves, and thereby created particular strategies and banks of knowledge both about the subject and how to understand it.

But post-democracy, many of these reporters were burnt-out and eager for change and so moved out of the reporting of political violence. The newsroom returned to "normal", violence-related journalism was given to the crime reporter and knowledge and techniques gained by the conflict reporters were not incorporated into how to handle the present-day complexities of reporting violence, despite the fact that much of the violence of the times bore frightening similarities to the apartheid-era attacks and massacres in KwaZulu-Natal. Post-1994, as newsrooms in South Africa struggled mightily with "transformation" and the attempt to engage broader audiences among those who had been previously excluded from media, a constant question and discussion topic was the escalating violence, the reporting of it and the readers' saturation and frustration with it. In these days there was a high expectation of calm and peace and ongoing reporting of conflict served to confuse both journalists and readers who expected that the roots of the conflict (apartheid) had been dealt with and so the evidence of conflict all-round was an inexplicable occurrence.[17]

In December of 1998 I attended a conference organised by the Media Peace Centre in Cape Town, in conjunction with Media Action International, which focused on violence in areas of the world recognised as undergoing serious conflicts. On the agenda was discussion and debate about Bosnia, Rwanda and Burundi, Liberia, East Timor, Northern Ireland and Afghanistan. One of the most fascinating inputs came from local psychologist Dr Gordon Isaacs who worked at the Trauma Centre for Survivors of Violence and Torture. As a result of his work at the time with witnesses appearing before the Truth and Reconciliation Commission, he was invited to give his insights on how media foster trauma through reporting.[18] He offered the opinion that reporting death and disaster can create trauma by making audiences into vicarious participants and speculated that the pervasive feeling at the time that South Africans were shutting out and avoiding news reports about rising criminality, was because they felt traumatised by the journalism they were exposed to.[19] He listed the symptoms as the same ones that people living in war zones would be experiencing: guilt, helplessness, losing one's positive sense that life has worth and starting to despair.[20]

This was a very interesting connection: that the violence of so-called criminality was equivalent in effect to the violence of other types of conflict, and that the media role in conveying trauma through reporting could be equivalent in both situations.

While the conference rightly spent the majority time focusing on the responsibility of journalists to evaluate their roles in highly-charged and dangerous war zones, it opened up the possibility to ask whether ordinary beat reporting of crime and courts in a violence-ridden society, should not be subjected to the same scrutiny as war journalism.

At the 1998 conference the various media organisations attending made an appeal for a new approach to journalism – "peace journalism"[21] – instead of "objective" journalism guided by the news values of conflict, size, disaster and impact as seen from an elite point of view. This brand of journalism has some important hallmarks:

- It takes seriously that media reports have impacts and that these can very negatively affect conflicts. Hannes Siebert, then of the Media Peace Centre, said: "Working on numerous conflicts on the continent [Africa] over the last 10 years, it has become very clear that we, the media, impact whether we intend to or not. We impact in spite of ourselves."[22]

- It takes a pro-peace and pro-de-escalation of conflict stance, and asserts that in a conflict journalists should act consciously in the interests of peace, not by becoming conflict mediators but by practising a different kind of journalism.

- It takes issue with objectivity as an excuse for not taking this stance and asserts that every journalist in a conflict is a situated human being with a position, and not a neutral channel of information.

According to Robert Karl Manoff, Director of the Centre for War, Peace and the News Media at New York University: "No single issue has so bedevilled the discussion of media and conflict as the deeply held belief on the part of many journalists that the very idea of media-based preventative action violates the norm of objectivity – whose corollary, disinterestedness with respect to the events being reported, is an essential element of the professional creed. Objectivity is both necessary and impossible. It is a 'vital illusion'– and perhaps even a tragic one. Objectivity is unobtainable but the effort to achieve it is much of what gives the practice of journalism its social utility and undoubted nobility. Despite this nobility, objective journalism may be faulted on the grounds that its epistemological strength as a truth-seeking technique is also the source of a fundamental moral weakness."[23]

And what is this "moral weakness" Manoff is referring to? Johan Galtung says the dominant view operating in news journalism "sees conflict as a battle, as a sports arena, or gladiator circus. The parties, usually reduced to two, are combatants in a struggle to impose their goals... war journalism has sports journalism and court journalism as its models". But, he also says, "In conflict there is also a clear opportunity for human progress, using the conflict to find new ways, transforming the conflict creatively so that the opportunities take the upper hand – without violence." This is an important point to hold on to. Conflicts, because of their inherent volatility, hold within themselves the possibility for transformation, and this transformation could be positive as well as negative. Peace journalism as a practice insists that journalists use their communicating power for the positive outcomes to gain the upper hand.

Galtung challenges journalists to replace traditional news values with a different set of values which further the interests of negotiation, dialogue, resolution and peace. This entails:[24]

- Humanising all participants in the conflict and not demonising one side as "evil". But where lies, propaganda and wrong-doing are uncovered, reporting them without favouring one party or construing one set of wrong-doing as more evil than another set.

- Giving voice to all parties – and thereby recognising that media plays a vital communication role in allowing those not in dialogue to hear each other speak.

- Highlighting initiatives to end conflict; ideas and solutions; focusing on areas of strength and creativity.

- Focusing on the ordinary people and their ingenuity and efforts to transform the conflict.

Jake Lynch, another proponent of peace journalism who has written on the friction between immigrant communities and native Britons[25], adds the following aspects[26]:

- Illuminating structural and cultural violence as part of the explanation for violence.

- Framing conflicts as consisting of many parties pursuing many goals – a "cat's cradle" rather than "tug of war".

- Making visible peace initiatives and solutions, whoever suggests them.

- Distinguishing between stated positions and real goals, when judging whether particular forms of intervention are necessary or desirable.

This kind of journalism moves away from "win or lose" and the focus on the actions of the elite with power which render everyone else suffering the effects of the conflict as powerless.

Pushing the point further: Galtung makes an interesting comparison to the reporting of disease and death. We do not call reporters covering this territory "disease journalists" but "health journalists", and our assumption is that health is the normal state which their journalism helps people to move towards. But we do talk about "war reporting" and "war correspondents" with the assumption that war is a natural state for human beings and we do not believe that such journalists have a responsibility to help us move towards peace. "Changing the discourse within which something is conceived, spoken of and acted upon is a powerful approach," Galtung remarks.[27]

To return to my preoccupation about the need to examine our underlying assumptions and whether peace journalism has applicability for reporting all forms of violence in society: John Hartley from Queensland University of Technology says this even more strongly, when he talks about what "journalists think and do".

"Their occupational ideology is founded on violence, which is a *primary theory* of journalism for practitioners. Its basic thesis is that truth is violence, reality is war, news is conflict. It's not just a theory either – it's a desire. The *demand* of the reading public, the need for democratic accountability and the ideal type of the journalist all converge in a passion for conflict. If journalism is a 'profession' at all then it is the profession of violence.

"Journalism's heroic figures are the combative interviewer who won't take no for an answer, the war junkie following death around the world, the adversarial investigative reporter, the crusading paper or programme. The good journalistic watchdog fights for stories that someone doesn't want told; the best stories are those that expose violence and corruption concealed within respectable institutions, from tin-pot dictators to children's homes. Journalism is combat."[28]

South Africa as a newly-created society has come out of a multi-faceted life or death struggle in which the conflagration of an entire country was an ever-present possibility, and at that point in our history the uncovering of the roots of violence was crucial and had a self-evident justification. But now that same society is finding it very difficult to reconcile itself to a journalism which has the seeking out and magnification of violence at its heart without good justification. While the apartheid-related violence carried a powerful rationale for reporting – recording the atrocities of the regime for history and showing the inventiveness of the struggle against it; what rationale is there for telling a new democracy that its basic structures of law and order are powerless against a new type of monster criminal (the revolutionary turned bad) and that daily the new land is in a fragile and precarious state?

If journalists in South Africa are going to abandon a brand of journalism that has a certain type of conflict at its heart and is accompanied by an ideology of neutralism, then an investigation of what the present conflict is and how it works criminally and politically is important. A useful framework to inform this discussion comes from the research of the Centre for the Study of Violence and Reconciliation (CSVR) based in

Johannesburg, which has for years studied and reported on the forms of violence and conflict emerging in post-apartheid South Africa.[29]

Graeme Simpson, executive director of the CSVR, makes several extremely useful and pertinent points about conflict and violence in present-day South Africa. These are:

- That the South African transition from apartheid to democracy has been "romanticised". 'Political' violence – the kind suffered by mainly black South Africans as a direct exercise by the apartheid state – is now thought to be securely in the past. He puts this neatly when he talks about the "erroneous assumption that South Africa – as a consequence of the formal enfranchisement of black South Africans who were previously denied political rights – is a 'post-conflict' society".

- South Africa is ridden with conflicts of multiple kinds, at many different levels of society. It remains an extremely violent country with violence used in many ways to achieve all sorts of social, political, personal and economic goals. In fact, transition has heightened particular types of conflict and not diminished them. 'Criminal' violence has surged since 1994 and Simpson remarks: "...the circumstances of civil war in apartheid South Africa breathed life into a resilient violence-based sub-economy rooted in the trade in arms, assassination and protection in which there were extensive vested material – rather than merely political – interests."

- The nature of conflict has changed – but conflict has not gone away as a result of the vote. "Civil society in South Africa has remained highly militarised, chiefly manifesting in the form of violent crime and private justice and security, simply because... gross poverty and inequity – the structural underpinnings of marginalisation and violence in South Africa – have not yet been ameliorated."

- Violence has been "relabelled": now all violence is considered 'criminal' when in fact – before transition – 'political' violence was not without its criminal content. Simpson says the TRC fostered this "narrow" view of violence by setting up its hearings and committees in such a way that they drew boundaries around 'political' violence and refused to give amnesty or allow hearings that dealt with violence not considered 'political'. "The prevalent violence of everyday social life finds little complex expression here [in a simple, political narrative] ignoring the extent to which the criminalisation of politics and the politicisation of crime have been – and still are – two edges of the same sword."

• Those blamed for today's 'criminal' violence – young, black men – are the same social group involved in the "slide that was often made by young marginalised men between involvement in political and criminal violence... in fact the experiences of marginalisation and alienation that shaped much of young men's engagement in political organisation and the violence of liberation during the 1970s and 1980s, remains largely unchanged and consequently underpins the sustained involvement of these young men in criminal gangs in the post-1994 period".

• And finally, the awful truth encapsulated in this view of violence: societies in major transition are full of violence; the violence transmutes and blurs the lines between political, criminal and social despite attempts to separate out these factors by analysts and politicians. Simpson suggests that an accommodation must be made which accepts that ongoing conflict in South Africa is "inevitable" and cannot be "ended or negotiated out of existence".

A simple paradigm of conflict resolution is not sophisticated enough to deal with this blurred and endemic violence; it requires the "rebuilding of the social fabric" ... "a strengthening ... of the organs of civil society" and "tackling the roots of such changing violence both in the state and in civil society".

It is this understanding of conflict that I am going to employ in focusing on the challenges for South African news media today. But I also want to point out that the conflation of the terms 'violence' and 'conflict' in much of South African journalism is problematic. "In a lot of reporting, conflict is used to mean violence. Understanding the difference is crucial ... conflicts can be positive and constructive by opening avenues of change if managed effectively."[30]

There is no doubt that a society in major transition from authoritarianism to a rights-based culture would be full of conflict, but it is South Africa's levels of violence and their impacts – not only on citizens – but on the process of creating a robust democracy that requires that the situation be understood and responded to with greater sophistication.

And to return to the challenge posed by peace journalism to take a stance, should journalists in South Africa not adopt a conscious position which is pro-building a robust civil society; pro the strengthening of democratic institutions; pro the ordinary citizen being empowered with information and choices, and abandon "objective journalism" based on a false disinterest?

To bolster this argument I am going to reach back in time and look at two seminal processes in which the news media was placed under scrutiny and which highlight its activities while embracing a position of neutrality; traditional news values and objectivity.

The Truth and Reconciliation Commission and the Media

If we take Simpson's observation about the simple split between pre-democracy 'political violence' and post-election 'criminal violence', and use it purely for the purposes of gauging how the news media acted to report apartheid-generated violence which was clearly understood as 'political', what does this say about the functionality of the objective journalism paradigm?

Under apartheid the media not directly controlled by the apartheid state (such as the South African Broadcasting Corporation) could legitimately claim a draconian level of control over their practices and products. South Africa, pre-1994, could not in any way be considered a nation in which freedom of expression was a norm[31]. Reporting the violence meted out by the apartheid state and getting at the stories of 'political' violence was extremely difficult: only when such violence found its way into the criminal records or courts (or was referred to by members of parliament in the privilege of that house of government) could it be made official enough to report on through normal journalistic means. But it is revealing that when the Truth and Reconciliation Commission focused a series of special hearings in 1997 on the media and asked the question about whether they had "created the climate" for apartheid, a number of issues were raised that had nothing to do with oppressive laws and controls.

Putting aside the apartheid practices perpetrated by media houses on their own employees (and several submissions to the commission dealt precisely with these), and putting aside the infiltration of state spies into the business of news, what was highlighted was that the inherited paradigm of objective, "just get the facts" journalism was itself a factor that hindered the circulation of important information publicly. Much of the TRC's attention was focused on the English-language press which considered itself oppositional to the apartheid regime. The Afrikaans press was solidly pro-Nationalist Party (or even further to the right), and the public broadcaster was controlled to such an extent by the government that it was in breach of the laws set up to help it operate.[32] In his submission, former editor of the *Rand Daily Mail* Raymond Louw told the hearing: "White journalists were not anti-apartheid activists. Their job was to uncover the truth and to print it. Black journalists were activists first."[33] In other words those who wanted to be 'objective' journalists could not also act as citizens of a country engulfed in a civil war, and those who tried to prioritise the political violence in their reporting risked being branded as dangerous radicals in the newsrooms and put into safer beats where they could not attract the notice of the police. "The commission asked the publishing houses to address, at the hearing, the issue of how their publications covered the violence. Unfortunately this was not adequately done. For example, the manner in which the media covered the violence, possibly because the casualties were usually black, did not always convey how desperate the situation was."[34]

Another extremely insightful comment came from the then president of the mostly white SA Union of Journalists, Sam Sole who said: "There is a lack of a common intellectual framework for what we do as journalists. We are victims of our violent history and the denigration of intellectual activity."[35] This denigration of the intellectual took the form of not interrogating the media's own activities and standpoints on apartheid. "The racism that pervaded most of white society permeated the media industry."[36]

The Media Monitoring Project remarked in its submission to the TRC that journalists "continued to report within the social and economic discourse defined by the apartheid state. The state legitimated itself within that discourse, and by not challenging its centrality or providing significant oppositional utterances to it, the English press wittingly or unwittingly validated the apartheid state." The commission went on to comment: "Thus, even though some of the media may have opposed the government, the social and political system created by apartheid was sanctioned by the media. The media analysed society from inside that system and did not provide alternative perspectives or discourses from the outside."[37]

In its final report[38] the TRC said: "The commercial newspaper industry had it origins in colonialism and was modelled on its British equivalent.

From the early 20th century, mining capital played an increasingly dominant role in the newspaper industry… the publishing houses reflected the broader apartheid structures. Ownership was exclusively white. The term 'opposition press', used to describe the English-language press, was a misnomer. Within this bi-polar world, there was only one viewpoint propounded in the mainstream press and that was a capitalist perspective. Independent, black, liberal, socialist and communist publications were either banned or folded under commercial pressure, while the so-called mainstream press prospered and grew."

So there it was. Despite "periodic flashes of courage and brilliance"[39] the news media was mired in its own racism, and so invested in a discourse of race, inequality, and the need for draconian control and security, that it could not see the need to examine its own belief-system, practices and resultant products. In this case the stance of neutrality and objectivity fed directly into the existing racialised world constructed by the apartheid regime and did not unmask its illegitimacy.

As a result of the commission hearings and the consequent very public discussion, the newly formed South African National Editors' Forum, set up a discussion with journalism trainers to talk about the state of the profession in 1997. A task group was asked to focus on and put forward recommendations on whether the country needed a "new paradigm" for journalism. It was noted that journalism as practised under apartheid and still in 1997 had the following hallmarks:

- It was Eurocentric[40] and authoritarian.

- It was fragmented into content areas and gave little context to events.

- It was reactive and not reflective – in the sense of thoughtful, interpretive.

- It held to the powerful, pervasive view that it was a 'mirror on society' and as such non-ideological, providing facts without point of view.[41]

- It considered itself as presenting 'balance' in contentious stories – presenting issues as having two sides only: pro and con.

- Its attitude was to supply information only, without making the connections to communities, resulting in stories without relevance.

- There was little recognition of different audiences.

- Stories were being dictated by powerful sources and not receivers.

- Ownership monopolies and 'bottom-line dictates' practices were prevalent.

- There was a general lack of situatedness in the wider world and Africa[42].

The task group recommended that the shift to a 'new paradigm' be given attention by both educators and editors. They said it should take seriously:

- The connections media can make between their audiences, society, the country, Africa and the wider world and that these connections should be explicitly made in the journalism.

- The need for a consciousness of diversity – in newsrooms (by acknowledging the variety of contributions that could be made) and in audiences and their needs.

- There should be emphasis on context, interpretation, research, investigation, 'complete' reporting and analysis.

- The use of sources should move beyond the 'authorities'.

- Media ownership needed to be diverse and involve multiple stakeholders.

It was clear to those paying attention that what was evident from the TRC hearings was that journalism itself was under investigation and not simply journalists and their behaviour during the apartheid state. A year later a group of South African journalists were invited to talk about the TRC experience to East and West German journalists in Berlin. I concluded in the talk I delivered then: "There is no doubt in my mind the media were complicit. Apartheid thrived because of the kind of reporting that happened in this country. It wasn't just a matter of draconian legislation, of laws and danger and repression. It was also how we the journalists understood what we were doing and who we were doing it for. If we start to redefine what a story is, what its purpose is, how it speaks for a person and for a nation, and how it contributes to shared knowledge and understanding, then we start to redefine journalism."[43]

A very worrying aspect of the interrogation of the media and the reporting of the past violence was that it did not underline strongly enough the role of subconscious racism as the major contributing factor. Simpson speaks of "failing to adequately scrutinise racism as entrenched institutional (and often violent) practice embedded in the fabric of South African society".[44] He relates this failure to the TRC process in general and to the present government's activities, but it is as valid to apply this to the news media and its operations, then and now. Although the TRC did find practices of racism prevalent in the newsrooms and structures of media organisations, the commission did not point to racism as a key area for journalists to beware of in the future as regards the story-telling they practise and the standpoint from which they do this.

The Human Rights Commission and the Media

When the Human Rights Commission held two weeks of special hearings into racism in the media in the year 2000, it picked up and pushed further this theme. It probed for attitudes, practices and effects perpetuated by the news media that feed into the ongoing inequality and discrimination that continue to be part of daily life in South Africa for all but the most privileged of those without white skins. The hearings were sparked by complaints from professional bodies of black lawyers and business people who remarked that the watchdog function of the news media seemed to be aimed directly at undermining the new black government of the country. The complaints were aimed particularly at the *Mail&Guardian* and the *Sunday Times* but were widened by the HRC to focus on all news media. At the same time there was widespread public debate about the number of stories on corruption and crime, which seemed to focus particularly on actions by the new civil servants coming into central and provincial government service.

After submissions by nearly every significant media institution in the country the HRC released a report[45] saying: "To the extent that expressions in the South African media 'reflect a persistent pattern' of racist expressions and content of writing ... South African media can be characterised as racist institutions... racism cannot and must not be equated simply with bad journalism. What makes for bad journalism is hardly ever the racist content or effect of a particular copy...We are concerned that a too easy resort to an explanation of bad journalism, might be another form of evasion and denial of racism."

Going to the mindset of South African journalism the HRC commented: "Much racism occurs at the institutional or structural level. It occurs as historical reliance is made on common sense methods and systems without interrogating what messages these convey about the cultural diversity of our country, about the history of inequality and about the dominant knowledge systems that create a unipolar view of the world."

On the new Constitution and guiding framework for all of South African life the HRC commented: "Very few newspapers attested to placing our Constitution and Bill of Rights at the centre of their professional consciousness and responsibility. Again and again, we were told that no formal training on the Bill of Rights was available to new recruits and no check on the application of the Bill of Rights to the work of journalists was encouraged. …the fact that present monitoring frameworks are only re-active and no investigation can be conducted at the instance of the self-regulatory body, is a serious flaw in the current system."

The commission then outlined the following as areas needing attention:
- Journalists at all levels of the industry need racism awareness training and educational institutions should consider modules on racism in their training.
- Exposure of journalists to the cultural diversity that forms the fabric of our society should be promoted.
- Journalists need workshops on the Bill of Rights and Promotion of Equality and Prevention of Unfair Discrimination Act 2000 which focuses on the prohibition of racism and the promotion of equality and human dignity. An understanding of the Constitution and human rights needs to be integrated into training of student and cadet journalists.
- There should be ongoing public debate about the role and responsibility of the media in a democracy.

Again for those paying attention it was clear that adherence to a narrow, scripted form of inherited Western-style journalism that espouses objectivity as its core value without any consciousness of its situatedness in complex webs of racial domination and western hegemonic world views, was – at best – resulting in an inadequate job of reporting a society in major transition. At worst it was helping to perpetuate the inequalities of a society that the new democracy was intended to move away from.

Both the TRC and HRC hearings into the media – although greeted with annoyance by many in the media as an expensive waste of time – have been important markers on the road to a better functioning democracy.

Both commissions are organs of the new democratic state put in place precisely to beef up and make more robust this new experiment in transition. Both commissions – for those paying attention – highlighted that the ongoing conflict in this country is directly related to race-based actions and violence that despite transition to a popular democratic system, continue to underlie many social structures and institutions in South Africa today.

If journalists operating in this country take seriously the findings and recommendations of the TRC and HRC, if they pay attention to the debates being conducted in bodies like the SA National Editors' Forum, if they eavesdrop on the discussions by trainers and educators, if they pay heed to debates across the world[46] – then the conclusion must be reached that embracing a more nuanced, more sophisticated, more listening, more flexible form of news journalism is critical and urgent.

That is the big overarching task for journalism as a practice and profession. But focusing more narrowly on the task at hand – that of reporting successfully the new forms of conflict and violence that have sprung up in South Africa post-apartheid, direction must be found to re-orientate journalistic practice. I would like to suggest that peace journalism could be investigated as a practice offering a different attitude, approach and stance. I would also like to suggest that given the general crisis facing journalism as an entire profession, for journalists covering the levels of violence and the range of conflict in South Africa today, to lean on the old, tried and trusted methods of courts and crime reporting is to inadequately get at the underlying story of what is really going on in our society.

To reduce conflict to the arenas of crime and courts is to embrace that simplistic dualism Simpson outlined: that pre-democracy violence was 'political', and post-elections the violence is 'criminal' and the world we inhabit is now a 'post-conflict' one. Merely tracking the violence through the catalogues of crime (usually via the police and their statistics-gathering processes) or through the courts, results in a journalism that is a-contextual, full of mind-bewildering numbers, and is laden with the salacious details gleaned from horrific and extraordinary violence (in the grand tradition of one more murder is not news unless it has some gruesome unusual component).[47] The result of this kind of reporting – which sits solidly within the framework of objective, factual reporting and its attendant news value system[48] – is that it is widely perceived to be undermining the project of building a new nation. It is divisive, with many black South African politicians holding the view that the news media continue to be "white-owned"[49] and to have a stake in watch-dogging the black government out of power.

To return to Robert Karl Manoff: "Human beings have a great need to understand the truth of things. (It could even be argued that we actually do not appreciate the full extent of what might be called our 'species-need' for truth.) To put it another way: truth has survival value for individuals, economies and polities. Whatever its failures and illusions, objectivity-based journalism has proven to be an effective technique for seeking our species-truth. However, objectivity may be only that: a particular technique. In fact, objective journalism, which we often represent to ourselves as an enduring value… is only a half-century old. In other words, in discussing 'media and conflict' issues, it is important not to fall prey to an a-historical essentialism that presumes that today's form of journalism is, or ought to be, tomorrow's. …Contemporary journalism is in flux. The intensity of the debates over issues such as multiculturalism and public, civic and community journalism signal to us that the future of the profession is very much up for grabs."[50]

Whatever opinions consumers hold of South African TV news bulletins, the newspapers or the radio stations, they are still using the news media to figure out what is going on in the world and how to negotiate it. It may even be that the annoyance and anger with the coverage of critical issues (Aids, crime, politics, economics) is driven by the expectations South African audiences and readers have for valuable and important information that they can trust and use to direct their lives.

I would like to suggest a number of things about the shift needed in how we practise our journalism in this country:

1. That the ongoing introspection which involves understanding the paradigm which historically underlies the practice of journalism in this country is a necessity and should not be treated as a simple moment in the confessional from which we move on rapidly.

2. That we also examine that journalism as a business turns on the amount of conflict in the world and uses it as the nutrient to feed a very competitive and commercially-rapacious industry. That this conflict is often treated salaciously and without much thought as to the damaging effect it has on the psychological ability of the ordinary citizen to feel

safe, secure, in control and as someone who has agency in a complex world.

3. That it is critical for the news industry to commit itself unequivocally to the values of the Constitution and the Bill of Rights. And that this standpoint should be made visible and audible and thereby replace the undeclared situation in which neutrality and objectivity is assumed but which in actuality is a cover for an unspoken vote for capitalism, liberal democracy and unregulated freedom of expression which applies to only those with media power.

4. That media managers in South Africa stop assuming that the task is simply widening the net to include those previously excluded from media consumption or to make newsrooms more reflective of the demographics of the population. It is not about more of the same for more people but about allowing different audiences to speak loudly about different kinds of media and what kind of news they would like for their purposes. It is about moving from the assumption (underscored by an undeclared allegiance to the capitalist market) that our readers and audiences are "consumers" and instead treating them as "citizens" – all involved in the project of building a new democracy.[51]

5. That the shift is also about questioning the assumption that a free press – regardless of its shape or colour or preoccupations – is inherently a pillar of democracy and asking ourselves what it would take to build news media that would be a positive force for democracy. If news media want to be commercially successful industries then they can go ahead and do whatever they want to please their consumers regardless of public opinion, but if they simultaneously claim the moral high ground of being the "Fourth Estate" and speaking to government with an authoritative voice on behalf of the public, then they must pay attention to what the public demands of them in this role and be willing to be accountable to that same public for how they play this role.

6. And that we need to continue to take racism very seriously as an underlying force for much of the violence we see but being more creative about speaking about it and making it evident. South Africans have a very low threshold for talking about racism, it is the primary subject for confinement to the past, and so a conversation about racism needs to be cleverly crafted for it to be useful. In this case journalists

need to abandon the position that "denigrates the intellectual" (in the words of Sam Sole, now working as a correspondent for the *Mail&Guardian*) and start paying attention to the work of academics, media theorists and researchers. This work is a source not only of subjects but injects different modes of analysis into what are mostly common sense debates on these fraught issues between news media and public. There is no doubt also that the public needs access to different ways of thinking about these issues and that many of the fearful and entrenched positions[52] held in public could benefit from the challenge of better informed points of view.

In conclusion, the complexity and inexplicability of the violence of South African life cries out for a journalism that is more probing, more analytical, more enabling for citizens to make sense of. The paradigm inherited from the British media, perfected by the US, and practised broadly across the world by the mainstream news media has shown itself at two particular points in our recent history to have serious flaws in getting at our "species-need for truth". We would do well as journalists not to shut down the debate now and hurry rapidly on from the embarrassing point where we have had to account to two commissions for our past behaviour. We should open up the conversation to all who have a stake in the news media playing a critical role in the building of our new democracy.

To return to Robert Karl Manoff in his essay on the task facing US journalism post 9/11. Referring to news media workers as "citizen-journalists", he says: "...journalism has no meaning apart from the democracy that is its *telos* – its grounds for being, the *end* whose achievement demands the pursuit of journalism as an ambitious undertaking in the public sphere."[53]

Notes
[1] www.mtncpc.co.za

[2] The South African Law Commission says: "The prevalence of child abuse in South Africa is staggering: in 1996 the Child Protection Unit of the SAPS alone dealt with 35,838 cases of crimes against children, which represents an average increase of 36% per year since 1993." www.pangaea.org/street_children/africa/safrsex.htm

[3] "Comparing South Africa's murder rate to those of other countries suggests that South Africa is indeed one of the most dangerous countries

in the world..." The Institute for Security Studies www.iss.co.za/CJM/ CRIMEINSA.HTML

4 www.iss.co.za/CJM/SpecificCrimesinSA/CarTheft.html

5 www.iss.co.za/CJM/SpecificCrimesinSA/AgraRobbery.html

6 Crime Busters of SA ,which has a vested interest in this issue, makes the following claims on its website (www.100megspop2.com/crimebusters/ FarmVictims.html): that the murder rate stands at 313 per 100 000 population and that from 1991 more than 1700 of SA's 40 000 farmers, farmworkers and their families have been killed. The SA Police Services' Crime Information Analysis Centre (www.saps.org.za/ 8_crimeinfo/farm99/index.htm) says: "Efforts aimed at curbing the escalating wave of attacks on farms and smallholdings have thus far failed in their aim."

7 The ISS comments: "Vigilantism has become a widespread and serious concern for government and civil society. The problem is hard to quantify, but the largest and most recent survey conducted in 1999 in the Eastern Cape found that 1 in 20 people said they had personally been involved in vigilante activity." www.iss.co.za/CJM/ SpecialInterest/Vigilantism.html

8 Police statistics reported by the Centre for the Study of Violence and Reconciliation (www.csvr.org.za/papers/papvtp4.htm). "Despite government efforts to regulate and clean up the industry, tensions and killings continue every year." www.iss.co.za/CJM/SpecialInterest/ TaxiViolence.html

9 See the study "Xenophobia: a new pathology for a new South Africa" by Bronwyn Harris at www.csvr.org.za/papers/paphar1.htm

10 *The New York Times* reported on 22 December 1998 that on Monday 21 December, Dlamini was attacked by a neighbour who ordered her to keep silent. That night, a group tore down her house and beat and stoned her, thus causing her death.

11 Prof. Thias Kgatla, a professor of theology at the University of the North, says the problem is so severe in the Northern Province that he has knowledge of five villages filled with nothing but ostracised "witches" and their families, quoted in a report by AP 30 October 1999 (accessed at www.rickross.com/reference/wicca/wicca22.html)

[12] www.gca.org.za/facts/briefs/47.htm

[13] www.iss.co.za/CJM/Performing.html

[14] The website "Come Home" is the face of an organisation set up deliberately to persuade highly-skilled emigrants to return to SA. Official statistics say that 65 000 emigrants have left the country since 1994 but, says Come Home, the true figure is probably closer to 400 000. The effects are that for the loss of each skilled person, 10 jobs are lost for unskilled people and each year the country loses R800-billion in tax contributions. www.comehome.co.za

[15] Masuku, S. (2003) "For Better and for Worse: South African Crime Trends in 2002", p24 in *SA Crime Quarterly* no 3 March 2003, Institute for Security Studies, Pretoria.

[16] Measured against the statistics from 90 other Interpol member countries, South Africa measures unacceptably high in violent crime, according to the Crime Information Intelligence Centre 2001 report (http://www.saps.gov.za/8_crimeinfo/200112/report.htm).

[17] For an extremely fascinating account of these times and the responses of various journalists based at *The Natal Witness* to the violence they were recording, see the PhD thesis by Lesley Fordred "Narrative, Conflict and Change: Journalism in the New South Africa" University of Cape Town January 1999. One particularly interesting approach to land-based conflict was adopted by reporter Donna Hornby, who practised a kind of "immersion journalism" by living for long periods in squatter camps and rural villages to give insight and depth to the stories she was writing.

[18] Report in *Rhodes Journalism Review* no 18 December 1999, "Witnessing Trauma: the Communication of Stress" by Anthea Garman, p40.

[19] A survey of the letters pages in the newspapers of the time bears witness to the irritation of many readers with the reporting of extreme violence.

[20] An interesting viewpoint to study alongside this is the work of George Gerbner, Dean Emeritus of the Annenberg School for Communications at the University of Pennsylvania. Gerbner's research into the reactions to violence screened on TV in the US shows that it has the effect not so much of creating a violent society, as a scared and fearful society

disposed to the use of draconian measures to keep it safe – a belief in the "mean world syndrome". "Contrary to usual popular conception, an inordinate amount of exposure to violent representations does not make people more violent. It makes people more insecure and fearful. In fact, it's great pacification and passivity training." (From an interview with New Dimensions www.newdimensions.org/NEW/online-journal/articles/saving-our-cultural.htm).

[21] This term is used by Johan Galtung. Director of Transcend, a global peace and development network. It is also spoken of as "Media intervention in conflict zones".

[22] Siebert, H. (1998) "Debunking the 'Big O'" p3 in *Track Two*, Vol 7 no 4 December 1998. Journal of the Centre for Conflict Resolution and the Media Peace Centre, Cape Town.

[23] Ibid

[24] Galtung. J. (1998) "High Road, Low Road" p7 in *Track Two*, Vol 7 no 4 December 1998.

[25] See his article "Responding to Difference" in *Rhodes Journalism Review* no 20, August 2001.

[26] Lynch's work on peace journalism can be found in two documents "Peace Journalism: how to do it" (www.transcend.org/PJOPTION.HTM) and "Reporting the World (www.transcend.org/reporting.htm).

[27] Galtung p9

[28] Hartley, J (1999) "Communicative Democracy in a Redactional Society: the Future of Journalism Studies" in *Journalism*, vol 1, no 1, Sage 2000.

[29] Simpson, Graeme. "Uncivil Society: Challenges for Reconciliation and Justice in South Africa after the Truth and Reconciliation Commission" at www.csvr.org.za/papers/papsim16.htm and "Rebuilding Fractured Societies: Reconstruction, Reconciliation and the Changing Nature of Violence – Some Self-Critical Insights from Post-Apartheid South Africa" www.csvr.org.za/paers/papundp.htm

[30] Lynch, J. and McGoldrick, A. in "Peace Journalism: How to do it" www.transcend.org/PJOPTION.HTM

[31] *TRC Final Report* Volume 4 Chapter 6, p188: "State restrictions on the freedom of the media played an important role in facilitating gross violations of human rights during the period covered by its mandate. These restrictions grew in intensity until more than 100 laws controlled the right to publish and broadcast."

[32] The Broadcast Act of 1976 required the SABC to "disseminate information" to "all the national communities … unambiguously, factually, impartially and without distortion." (Ibid p167)

[33] Quoted in Garman, A. "Fragments of the Truth" p30 in *Rhodes Journalism Review,* no 15, November 1997.

[34] *TRC Final Report* Volume 4 Chapter 6, p190

[35] Quoted in Garman, A. "Fragments of the Truth" p30 in *Rhodes Journalism Review,* no 15, November 1997.

[36] *TRC Final Report* Volume 4 Chapter 6, p189.

[37] Ibid p186.

[38] Ibid p173.

[39] Ibid p174.

[40] "Eurocentric" is South African shorthand for being influenced by the North, particularly the UK and US (and not necessarily Europe as the word would suggest).

[41] For an interesting take on the 'mirror' metaphor, Hannes Siebert comments: "I am not sure why supporters of the 'mirror' argument prefer to ignore the shapes or angles of these mirrors… these shapes are determined by one's worldview, one's understanding of a particular situation/event or conflict, one's capacity to capture the complete picture, one's sense of responsibility towards the people one reports on or for and, very importantly, by the medium one uses." p3 *Track Two* Vol 7 no 4 December 1998.

[42] See "A New Paradigm for Journalism in South Africa" p 15 in *Rhodes Journalism Review* no 15 November 1997.

[43] Garman, A. "The TRC and the Story", Media Dealing with the Past Seminar Berlin, 29 November 1998.

[44] Simpson, Graeme. "Uncivil Society: Challenges for Reconciliation and Justice in South Africa after the Truth and Reconciliation Commission", www.csvr.org.za/papers/papsim16.htm

A further point to be taken into account is that the TRC focused on the extreme manifestations of racism by cataloguing "gross violations" of human rights. It did not hear from millions upon millions of average black South Africans denied liveable housing, access to jobs and services and given sub-standard education.

[45] South African Human Rights Commission report "Faultlines: Inquiry into Racism in the Media" August 2000. Section V "Observations, findings and recommendations".

[46] Just one international example: the challenge thrown up by newly-appointed President of Columbia University in New York, Lee Bollinger who questioned whether the "bootcamp"-style training that is the master's programme in journalism has a place in the university environment in the 21st century. (See the furious debate at rival New York University's website www.journalism.nyu.edu/pubzone/debate). In fact, journalism theorists world-wide are looking at journalism practice and questioning the way it operates – see the debates in *Journalism: Theory, Practice and Criticism,* Volume 1 Issue 1, April 2000, Sage.

[47] This leads to an ever-increasing horror scale: "rape of six month-old baby" topped by "rape of three-month-old baby".

[48] Galtung, J. and Ruge, M. (1981). "Structuring and Selecting the News" in Cohen, S. and Young, J. (eds.) London, Sage, 52-63.

[49] Despite evidence to the contrary with changes in ownership and leadership taking place so rapidly it is hard to keep track. But for a recent assessment of the national situation see the *Financial Mail* of 27 July 2001, pp50-51.

[50] Manoff, R. 1998. "Role Plays: Potential Media Roles in Conflict Prevention and Management" in *Track Two,* Vol 7 No 4 December 1998.

[51] One of the fiercest battles between Government and news media in South Africa post 1994 was the setting up of the Government

Communication Information Service in 1998. The news media construed this as a government propaganda arm to counteract the independence of the existing media. The Government impatiently told the editors that because of their entrenched ideas of what constitutes "news" they were not doing the job of telling the new citizens of the country the important but un-newsworthy information coming from institutions like Parliament which would allow them to make use of the benefits of new laws and regulations. This charge is absolutely true. The news media has nothing to gain financially in helping the recently disenfranchised figure out their new status in a new dispensation by filling valuable space/time with basic information about grants and rights.

[52] Espoused for example in the wide-spread call to "bring back the death penalty" and in the opinion that criminals have rights law-abiding citizens do not have (see the Crime Busters website for opinions of this sort).

[53] http://journalism.nyu.edu/pubzone/forum1.essay.manoff.html

3

The Triumph of 'Big Brother': Challenging Times for African Media in Conflict Situations

Simwogerere Kyazze

"[T] here is the alleged remark of the Nigerian who, after seeing a TV western, said delightedly, 'I did not realise you valued life so little in the West'" (McLuhan 1964:319).

This remark, though slightly off-colour, might help explain how Africans, long used to both oral tradition and the realism of game shows like traditional wrestling, would miss the point of acting in television film. The remark is credited to one of the most important media scholars of the 20th century, Marshall McLuhan, who went on to coin fabulous phrase after fabulous phrase. The most famous of all these fabulous phrases was of course the 'the global village'. Iconography aside, however, McLuhan's greatest contribution to existing knowledge was a serious interrogation of the effects of television on audiences. See, McLuhan wrote his best work in the 1960s, when television was just coming into its own as a medium of communication, replacing radio and challenging cinema as the pre-eminent source of entertainment in the United States. It helped of course that at the time, television was also increasingly becoming the main source of news for people; it was relatively cheap and involved only a one-off payment (to purchase the set) while it duplicated some of the best features of cinematic entertainment (Stephens 1997:280). In the Western world, no other medium is as loathed or as touted as television with regard to its social effects (Angus 1994:250).

Today, as in the past, television does not dominate the media landscape, but it somehow still dominates many of the mass media effects discourses since Marshal McLuhan and because of globalisation, the 'global village' is now made up of people who are exposed to the same universal culture beamed into their existence from Brazil to Australia, and from Finland to South Africa via global media conglomerates (Moran 1998:3).

The latest development in visual media is reality television, a format launched in 1996 by John De Mol, a former radio DJ in Holland who thought the idea of placing carefully selected people in a sealed-off house and beaming their every utterance, action and inaction would be captivating (*The Daily Telegraph* 2001). It was.

The success of reality television can be traced back to the same reason why peep shows and red-light districts are some of the biggest attractions in cities like New York and Amsterdam. There is apparently nothing to concentrate the mind quite like a live sex show— or the promise of one.

Of course, Mr De Mol views his Big Brother creation a little differently:

> The bottom line is that a lot of people consider their lives predictable and boring. This is something that gives them the opportunity to have the experiences they wouldn't normally have in 50 years. We know young people these days are only interested in fun, in 'what's in it for me' and excitement (*The Daily Telegraph* 2001:19).

Del Mol does confess however, that the shows he created are increasingly about sex and sexuality, have a jacuzzi and are contrived to have hot water only during particular times of the day, making showers at particular times almost compulsory, and creating for TV viewers what has been dubbed "shower hour" (*The Daily Telegraph* 2001).

An estimated 25 million viewers across Africa watched parts of the latest instalment of Mr Del Mol's 'peep show' called Big Brother Africa (*The Monitor* 2003:1). On May 25, 2003 Gaetano Kaggwa, a 31-year-old Ugandan law student, joined 11 young men and women from South Africa, Namibia, Mozambique, Botswana, Angola, Nigeria, Malawi, Ghana, Kenya, Zimbabwe and Zambia and they entered a specially built house where 27 cameras beamed their every move, including the shower scenes, to millions of eager viewers, 24 hours a day, for 106 days.

Up for grabs was a cash prize of US $100,000 for the last man or woman still standing (a lot of money in any language), and bits of fame and fortune for the rest. The winner, Cherise Makubale, 24, was determined on September 7, 2003, through a lottery involving viewers across Africa voting for their favourite housemate, using the short messaging Service (SMS) on their mobile phones and the internet. Before the final event, the 12 candidates had been whittled down to five through carefully contrived eviction procedures that involved the housemates nominating someone they wanted to leave the Big Brother Africa House, and the viewers across the continent voting out one of those with the highest nominations. The whole point of this reality show is to bring real-time interactivity between the 12 contestants and the millions of people who are watching them and to decide who should stay in and who should be evicted. In many ways, the contestants are putting on a show, with the viewers acting as the judges.

The Executive Producer of Big Brother Africa, Marie Roshold, argued in May that the show was a manifestation of the hunger among Africans for positive images of their continent and its people. Said Roshold: "Big Brother has proved to be a huge success in that the people we have chosen are breaking down stereotypes. They are creating dialogue across Africa" (*The Monitor* 2003:1).

Ms Roshold and others predictably tiptoed around the fact that the Big Brother Africa show also spoke volumes about its audience, and the fact that there is a certain morbid fascination with the sight of a naked human body in us all. Big Brother Africa essentially panders to the voyeur or 'Peeping Tom' in us all (Mulvey 2003:135). Many of us would love to secretly spy on a well-formed nude person, a fascination that "can only come from watching, in an active controlling sense, an objectified other" (Ibid: 135).

That might perhaps explain why Bruna Tatiana Lemas Estevão was the first person to be voted out of the Big Brother Africa House, after what viewers called her 'boring and prudish ways' of taking showers in her underwear and not doing it like other people, in the nude! Television's latest invention has apparently given everyone a respectable licence to bring the popcorn and claim to be watching normal fare television.

Make no mistake, either. The loquacious puritans notwithstanding, there were many Africans who loved watching Uganda's Gaetano Kaggwa having sex with South Africa's 25-year old Abergail Plaatjes in full view of 27 cameras (*Sunday Vision* 2003:1). Assertions by media managers like Molefe (2003) that African audiences only hunger for traditionally positive images of themselves do not sound as convincing:

> If negative material is consistently selected for a considerable period of time then a perception is deliberately created that only the negative exists and no positive, in the circumstances, is to be found. Source of content also addresses the question of allowing African voices to be heard. The continued use in some sections of our media of foreign

nationals as experts or commentators on matters affecting the continent entrenches the view that knowledge of scientific, economic and political developments is the exclusive preserve of these groups. Africans are merely portrayed as passive participants in the unfolding of their own story (Molefe 2003:2-3).

These media imperialism assertions, while legitimate to a certain extent, cannot hide certain facts about Uganda, however. The country is certainly no longer the despotic hellhole of the days of Idi Amin (Lamb 1990:78), or a complete economic shambles (Hansen and Twaddle 1991:21). Indeed, Uganda has been impressive in almost every sector since 1986, when Yoweri K. Museveni became president. Today, Kampala is routinely lionised for its positive outlook on inflation, governance, liberalisation, anti-corruption crusades, economic growth, and most impressively, its efforts against HIV/AIDS. Uganda's anti-HIV/AIDS strategy is regarded as the best in the world (UNDP 2003:215).

However, the country has also taken some knocks in the recent past, with accusations that it is hogging the political space (Mamdani 1995: 121), and behaving like a one-party regime in everything but name (Oloka-Onyango 2000: 43), with all the attendant problems of nepotism, corruption and intolerance. In addition, the country has faced a rebellion in northern Uganda since 1986, which has caused widespread loss of life and sapped the country's meagre resources in defence expenditure. Here is how Human Rights Watch describes the situation in the country:

> The Ugandan political landscape in 2002 was characterised by continued conflict over the "movement" system, by which Uganda is governed. As a result, political and civil rights were violated, though on a somewhat lesser scale than during the violent election year 2001. Uganda was a major player in armed conflicts in the region: Continuing during most of the year, the occupation by the UPDF (Uganda's army) of the north-eastern part of the Democratic Republic of Congo (DRC) began to be scaled back in September; meanwhile, the UPDF fought a major military offensive against the rebel Lord's Resistance Army in northern Uganda and southern Sudan. In both wars, civilians were victims of widespread abuse (Human Rights Watch 2003).

So, however much Pan African scholars assert the continent receives too much bad rap from Western media, the reality is that there is just too much bad news coming out of the African continent, Uganda inclusive.

For example, in a country where over 50 percent of the population is below 15 years (The Population Secretariat 1999), it might not be too difficult to see why younger people, especially those in urban areas that are relatively safe and affluent, are switching off. These young people are the manifestation of a reality that is giving media executives and journalism educators goose bumps; a reality that conflict is out and Big Brother Africa is in.

It is not just Big Brother Africa either. It is an entirely new feel-good culture—keen interest in goat races, celebrity gossip supplied under the 'Have You Heard' banner in *The New Vision*, the country's leading newspaper, sleaze and soft-porn in the more down-market *The Red Pepper,* as well as ample servings of sexual shenanigans and advice in 'Women & Men' from *The Monitor*. There is also Premier League from England, which is broadcast to Uganda via Supersport, one of 40-odd channels from Multichoice Africa, the pay television company from South Africa. The local subsidiary Multichoice Uganda has a particularly high return on capital premised on a direct South Africa-to-Uganda satellite rebroadcast model. It was established in 1995 and its advanced technology quickly positioned its flagship carrier, DSTv, as the only signal with countrywide reach, an enviable position it still enjoys to this day (Multichoice Africa 2003).

Between Multichoice, *The New Vision, The Monitor, The Red Pepper* and most of the FM radio stations in Kampala and other urban areas in Uganda, there is little time for people who were born in 1986 when President Yoweri Museveni came to power, to think about the more political dimensions of their country.

Instead, they will spend the weekend poring over a typical Saturday gossip page in Uganda's two leading national dailies below:

Daddy Stand Up - Museveni to Amos

There was father and son drama at the wedding of Nowomugisha Nzeire Kaguta, the younger half brother to President Museveni in Rwakitura last Saturday.

When President Museveni emerged from his house and took his seat next to his father Amos Kaguta, everybody stood up save for a few elderly ladies and Amos himself. That was understandable. However, 10 minutes later when the national anthem was being played, Amos still sat rooted to his chair. Slightly agitated, Museveni politely tapped him twice across the arm, beckoning him to stand up. Without reservation, the older Kaguta duly obeyed his son's instructions.

**

What Did Muhoozi Say?

There was fracas at the birthday party of Cedrick Babu, son of Capt. Babu, the State Minister for Housing, three weeks ago. At the party, a Kenyan invitee apparently did the unthinkable and sought to attack Major Muhoozi Kainerugaba, for claiming that a cow is man's best friend when it is said that the dog is. The Kenyan called Muhoozi very un-serious and stupid, which did not go down well with him. Muhoozi then assured the Kenyan asking him to step outside "just to talk."

Cedrick and Humphrey Nzeyi of Nandos intervened pleading with Muhoozi to let the matter rest – a plea which fell on deaf ears. The two went outside and talked, returning five minutes later with a smile. No one though knows what was said.

**

Wedding Bells

Little has been seen of former MP for Sheema North and World Bank Executive Alternate Director Richard 'Sir Rich' Kaijuka. However, eagle-eyed scouts spotted him and his wife last Sunday afternoon at Highway Take Away in Nyendo, Masaka where they had stopped off for a bite to eat. Scouts also say Sir Rich's family will host a lavish wedding at Munyonyo in January.

**

Muhwezi Kids in Retreat

There is much more to Susan Muhwezi than being a senior advisor to President Museveni on AGOA. Over the weekend, Susan ditched her job as an advisor and treated her children who were here on vacation from school in Turi to a retreat at Speke Resort Munyonyo. On the last day of their stay on Tuesday night, the whole group had dinner at The Stables Restaurant and were overseen by senior management of the resort who ensured all went well.

**

Onapito Chokes in Silk

Judging from his performance last Friday in Silk Royale, presidential press assistant Onapito-Ekomoloit doesn't know how to handle himself in a club. In the company of a number of babes, Ekomoloit took to the floor until modern technology stepped in.

As the DJ let out a plume of smoke (dry ice) onto the dance floor, choking and gasping for breath, Ekomoloit was forced to abandon his dance strokes and seek safety by the bar while struggling to contain his coughing fit!

**

Bukenya Sings on Capital

It appears that Vice-President Gilbert Bukenya is a man of many talents.

During a recording for his appearance on Capital FMs Desert Island Discs programme this Sunday at 7:00pm, when asked to pick his second song which was Katonda Yebale, Bukenya instead choose to sing the song. "He really can sing!" said Romeo Akiki, who is the producer of the show.

**

Entebbe Pros Hike their Service Fee

Entebbe has been swarmed with sex workers from Kampala since the DRC bound peacekeepers hit town. The pros have set up camp in Kitooro and roam the big hotels targeting the soldiers who dish between $50 and $200 for relief.

One pro who used to work in Kampala said a soldier gave her $190 (sh380, 000) for the one hour she spent with him in a major Entebbe hotel.

**

Bro for 1st Daughters

Impeccable sources tell us that the first daughters are deeply into Big Brother.

The trio – Natasha, Patience and Diana – get together every Sunday at one of their homes to watch the eviction and nomination. Patience likes Cherise because she is a typical African and is well behaved.

Our own Gae is also well liked by the trio but only because he is Ugandan and not because of the way he behaves in the house.

**

Saleh Given 'Kiboko'

At St. Emmanuel Cathedral in Rushere during the wedding of Nowomugisha Nzeire Kaguta last Saturday, Lt. Gen. Salim Saleh and myself were reprimanded for smoking within the church grounds! As we banged kaboozi over cigarettes, a reverend appeared from nowhere and in a hushed but firm voice told us to get out.

"Sinners can't smoke in the church grounds. Take yourselves and your cigarettes outside the boundary fence," the irate Rev told us. Feeling guilty Saleh and I took to the bushes to finish off our puffs.

**

Kabaka snubs FRELIMO

The whispers from Mengo are not encouraging. No sooner had Sylvia Nagginda who has been out of the country on a four week sojourn returned home than her husband, Kabaka Mutebi swiftly packed his bags and flew out under the cover of darkness which left one of his guests in a lurch. Kabaka was due to have met FRELIMO Secretary General Armando Guebuza for lunch last Tuesday, but was abruptly told "Kabaka is out." Hmm! (*The New Vision* 2003: 11).

The above servings show a newspaper that would hold its own in England where the royal family, David Beckham and wife Victoria 'Posh Spice', and music and movie celebrities are national obsessions. But there is something else going on. While in England David Beckham and his wife get equal treatment as objects of celebrity gossip, thereby making moot the point of gender discrimination, media in Third World countries generally, and in the specific case of Uganda, are still dominated by men, both as newsmakers and as captains of the media industry. The 'Have You Heard?' page above has got 10 stories, all largely of male representation, as if they do not get enough exposure in other news pages. There is the

President of Uganda, and his brother at a wedding, the President's son at a birthday party – all public events. There is the Kabaka (or King) of Buganda, the largest ethnic group in Uganda, apparently throwing a tantrum. There is the Vice President of Uganda singing on a radio talk-show. There is a planned wedding of the son of an Executive Director at the World Bank. And finally there is the deputy Presidential Press Secretary, Onapito-Ekomoloit, in a nightclub. In the three gossip stories about women on this page, a senior aide to the President is out at a picnic with her daughters, the President's three daughters are said to congregate in one of their homes to watch the reality television show Big Brother, and the last story is very typical: prostitutes increase the amounts of money they charge because of the influx of United Nations peacekeepers in the country.

For *The New Vision,* it is not enough that the President, his brother (who is a general in the army and commander of the National Reserve Force), his deputy, or his son (who is a major in the Uganda army and deputy commander of the Presidential Guard Brigade); for the newspaper, it is not enough that these authority figures dominate all other forms of news; they must be brought up in the gossip pages too. It seems almost as important to reinforce the women's traditional roles (going to picnics with children), domestication (the President's daughters) or the economic deprivation that forces them into crime (the prostitutes). It is not even clear what the newspaper, which is wholly government-owned, is trying to achieve by these details. But as Harris and Johnson (1965:57) have argued, "To recognise news is easier than to define it." But maybe the real question would be that as the government newspaper is reporting all these nice stories about the ruling elite, have they asked where the money the wedding the President is attending, came from?

Not to be left out, Uganda's only other national daily, *The Monitor* picks up where its competition stops:

Connie still a Stunner

She may not be Miss MTN anymore but Connie Nankya certainly is still a stunner. The size-8 beauty left many, but most of all MTN top marketing man Erik Van Veen, breathless with her dress at the dinner for newly crowned Miss Uganda Aysha Nassanga and Miss MTN 2003 Eva Asasira. And was her dress a bomb! It may not have been her day but she did steal the show. That black short number with a V-cut that revealed just enough flesh and leg did it all. Van Veen could not help himself. He was heard saying to her, "I like your dress."

**

Desree Finds Home at MFM

They say when one door closes, a window opens. This must be the case for Desree Barlow, former UTV news anchor and Capital FM presenter. Hardly has a month passed since Out & About reported that she had been shown the door at UTV (we don't know what happened at Capital FM) than she has landed herself a slot at Monitor FM. Also joining the crowd at the station is WBS's Jam Agenda presenter James Kazoora who is now driving us through every afternoon.

**

Couples Galore

It was quite different at Club Silk last weekend. The crowd was massive, and it seemed like it was an evening for couples. Rare appearances were made by Multi Choice's Gigi Magezi and her hubby Timothy who spent a fun-packed evening dancing away. The couple just had a baby recently, and were probably getting some relief from maternity/ paternity leave.

Then entered party animal Sofie Amako and Uganda telecom's Lorika Naburi who cosily stationed themselves at the far end. Renowned emcee Dennis' Matanda of Kaboozi ku Biri who initially looked bored and spent much of the evening watching Big Brother, finally sought the company of his date who came in late. The so-called dance maestro Roge was there too, in the company of a brown belle. And was that Chameleone we saw with Karitas?

**

Surveillance

Which new health club is that in Bweyogerere which shares a name with a popular sports bar in Nakasero and starts with a "J" where both male and female patrons use the same changing facilities with management giving the reason that the female changing facility is still under construction?

**

The Scramble for TID

You had to struggle to get noticed. Last Saturday, visiting Tanzanian musician TID of the Siamini fame, it was rumoured, would do a little entertaining for the crowds. Although he did turn up, he did not perform, much to the disappointment of the huge crowd. But his presence brought a lot of excitement to the ladies who were trying to get his attention. "Have you seen him?" "There, there," was what the keen Kampala babes whispered as they positioned themselves. And as for TID, he must have had healthy optical nutrition with a display of scanty outfits.

**

Gavin's 'Critical Assignment'

And we thought Garvin Seth had come in ready to rescue WBS's dying ShowTime Magazine! Well this "saviour" left us puzzled last week when he went to the airport to welcome Tanzanian musician TID without a tape in his camera. According to eyewitnesses, Seth left WBS all set but the excitement of having to travel in a limousine for the first time disorganised him. If forgetting his tape was not bad enough, Seth had no airtime to call office. So he begged one journalist to help him send an SMS. It was the Duty Free Shop which saved his day. He had to cough up a good amount of money to save face. That is how TID's arrival made it to WBS finally.

**

Following in Big Bro's Footsteps?

Weasel is slowly but surely following in his brother's footsteps. Not only does he dress like Chameleone, sing like him but he is also displaying a love for "blondes". Mbu he seems to have his mind set on having a "Dorotia" from another country by his side. Last Saturday while performing at Club Silk, Weasel gave more attention to one tantalisingly dressed blonde than all the other girls in the crowd. Leaving all the other babes visibly disappointed, he stuck it out singing for Mysterious Girl.

**

Was It Quarcoo's Living It?

Was it him or his look-alike? News reaching Out & About from Mombasa is that Patrick Quarcoo – or someone who looks very much like him – is living it on the romantic white sand beaches of Kenya's paradise. Just two weeks ago, the guy was spotted with his family chilling at Diani Beach near Jadini beach hotel. Now if that is not living luxuriously, what is it?

**

Paris Beckons Asea

You've got to hand it to this year's Miss Uganda 2003 first runner-up Barbara Asea. Not only did she manage to woo the crowd with her smile, intelligence and marvellous walk. Now we hear the gods have smiled on her and the catwalks of Paris are beckoning. Apparently she is first on Sylvia Owori's list of models who will soon fly to France to get introduced to modelling agencies and make it on the catwalks of Paris. Lots 'a luck gal (*The Monitor* 2003:17).

There is something peculiar about *The New Vision* and *The Monitor* gossip pages. Most of the stories are about men, a reproduction of a patriarchial representation of the world which is so common in African countries. According to Chabal and Daloz (1999), African media are not yet structurally ready to be more representative. As such, "…despite the current political 'democratic transitions' on the continent, there has been no modification in the notion of representation – firmly anchored as it is in the patrimonial system" (Ibid: 39). However there is also a manifestation of the apparent disconnect between the political establishment and Uganda's youth (16-30 year olds), who are the target and consumers of much of these cultural products.

McRobbie (2003:238) argues that much of what is happening is a rebellion by young people against the constraining lifestyles favoured by their older and more traditional parents/guardians/leaders. As she sees it, "commercial leisure enterprises with their illusion of freedom have, then, an attraction for youth" (Ibid: 239). The younger generations are often excluded from political discourse through age restrictions (most countries set 18 as the minimum age at which one can stand for and vote in an election), they are excluded from the media (many countries have laws that bar children, i.e. those under 18, from seeking employment), and from starting a family (in most countries anyone younger than 16 cannot get married). As such, the youth find creative ways of making themselves heard. And media executives, eager to cash in on this 'rebellion', are often only too happy to help them out.

So in 2003, we are witnessing George Orwell's 'Big Brother' syndrome being turned on its head. In a frightening peek into the future, Orwell (1952) predicted a time, specifically the year 1984, when the oppressors he so chillingly identified in another classic, *Animal Farm* (1972) would finally take away freethinking from human beings. The Englishman was worried that the cycle of oppression would be complete with the banning of books. It is 19 years since the world survived that particular catastrophe, but strangely, Orwell's thinking was not completely off the mark. What seems to have happened is the manifestation of the Orwellian nightmare without the predictable presence of a dictator banning books.

Huxley (1948) argued that by around the 26th century, human life would have advanced so much that it would be possible to create human life in laboratories; indeed that people would be so in love with their new technologies that they would be unable to think. Huxley's subtle, but equally powerful account, begins with a "Squat grey building of only thirty-four stories. Over the main entrance the words, CENTRAL LONDON HATCHERY AND CONDITIONING CENTRE, and, in a shield, the World State's motto, COMMUNITY, IDENTITY, STABILITY" (1948:1).

Postman (1985) finds a nexus between Orwell and Huxley with a declaration that the media have already won the war with human beings:

> What Orwell feared were those who would ban books. What Huxley feared was that there would be no reason to ban a book, for there would be no one who wanted to read one. Orwell feared those who would · deprive us of information. Huxley feared those who would give us so much that we could be reduced to passivity and egoism. Orwell feared that the truth would be concealed from us. Huxley feared that the truth would be drowned out in a sea of irrelevance. Orwell feared we would become a captive culture. Huxley feared we would become a trivial culture, preoccupied with some equivalent of the feelies, the orgy porgy, and the centrifugal bumblepuppy (Postman 1985: vii).

The anti-intellectualism that seems to be afflicting the world from Canada to Haiti, from Finland to South Africa, has begun to take a toll on political discourse, mostly because people lack both the relevant social knowledge and the ability to make their voices heard in the decision-making process (Angus 1994):

> The tendency of the most significant contemporary communication systems is to produce audiences without this capacity. Audiences tend to remain simply audiences; that is, communication systems tend to sever audiences from reciprocal production of social knowledge and engagement in decision-making (Ibid: 233).

This disconnect undermines democracy in America (Fallows 1996), but is particularly disastrous in the poorer countries of Africa like Uganda. In the one, democracy is over 220 years old; while in the other democracy cannot even be taken for granted in 2003, a generation after most African countries were freed from colonial rule. In other words, Americans can binge on MTV, advertising, 'Big Brother', 'Harry Potter', 'Survivor', 'Who Wants To Be a Millionaire?', 'The Matrix', etc, all they want. The state of their union might not be quite what its founding fathers envisioned, but there seems to be sufficient discourse going on over there to suggest that some of the best minds in academia and civil society want to reverse the slide (Yankelovich 1991). The groundswell of opinion, for example, saw the Reform Party candidate Ross Perot garner almost 20 million (or 19 percent) of the 100 million votes cast in the 1992 US Presidential elections (*Encyclopaedia Britannica* 2003). The terrorist attacks of September 11, 2001 have certainly concentrated minds about the threats to American ideals, however they define them. Added to the consolidation of economic and political ties in Europe, the awakening of an economic behemoth in China, we are looking at a radically different world from even five years ago. The one constant has been Africa, where:

> It is common on the continent to notice the greatest displays of luxury in an environment of poverty and squalor, most particularly in urban areas. Magnificent mansions sit square in the middle of slum areas. Gleaming white limousines make their way down dank and filthy alleys. Prosperously rotund businessmen mingle readily with dishevelled and dirty children...Wealth thus revealed is a symbol of their *collective prominence*, according to a process which we identify as 'vertical symbolic redistribution' (Chabal and Daloz 1999:42).

African media have their work cut out, faced with such odds, and the omens do not look good either. They can pretend that today's interest in

Big Brother Africa is akin to the blood lust of Roman times when gladiators faced off against one another or against beasts, for the amusement of emperors and their subjects. The spectacle did not stop the Roman Empire from finally collapsing, taking the mighty Latin language with it. Today's world is different from traditional African society, where most public activity was in front of crowds, like wrestling, fireside story-telling of fables and proverbs, *omweso* (African draughts), etc. The effects of modernity have put paid to many of these once beloved African 'spectacles.'

In their place is Big Brother Africa.

References

Angus, I. (1994) "Democracy and the Constitution of Audiences: A Comparative Media Theory Perspective" in Lewis J. and Cruz J. *Viewing, Reading, Listening: Audiences and Cultural Reception.* Boulder, CO: Westview Press.

Chabal, P. and Daloz, J.P. (1999) *Africa Works; Disorder As Political Instrument.* Bloomington IN: Indiana University Press.

Encyclopaedia Britannica. (2003). "Perot, Ross" Encyclopaedia Britannica Premium Service. http://search.britannica.com/eb/article?eu=60795 Accessed on Oct. 26, 2003.

Fallows, J. (1996) *Breaking the News: How the Media Undermine American Democracy.* New York, NY: Pantheon

Hansen, H.B. and Twaddle, M. (1991) (eds). *Changing Uganda.* London: James Currey

Harris, J. and Johnson, S. (1965). *The Complete Reporter* (2nd Edition). New York: Macmillan Co.

Human Rights Watch (2003) World Report 2003, Uganda http://www.hrw.org/wr2k3/africa13.html#defending. Accessed on Oct. 10, 2003

Huxley, A. (1948) *A Brave New World* London: Zodiac Press.

Lamb, D. (1990) *The Africans; Encounters from the Sudan to the Cape.* London: Mandarin

Mamdani, M. (1995) *And Fire Does Not Always Beget Ash: Critical Reflections on the NRM.* Kampala: Monitor Publications.

McLuhan, M. (1964) *Understanding Media: The Extensions of Man.* Cambridge, MA: The MIT Press

McRobbie A. (2003) "Feminism and Youth Culture" in Jermyn D. and Brooker W. *The Audience Studies Reader.* London: Routledge.

Molefe P. (2003) *News Coverage in Africa.* Presentation at Highway Africa, 2003. Rhodes University, South. Unpublished Manuscript.

Moran, A. (1998) *Copycat TV: Globalisation, Program Formats and Cultural Identity.* Luton, UK: University of Luton Press

Multichoice Africa, 2003), http://www.multichoice.co.za/map/Mapdetails.asp?CId=15. Accessed on Oct. 01, 2003

Mulvey, L. (2003) "Visual Pleasure and Narrative Cinema" in Jermyn D. and Brooker W. *The Audience Studies Reader.* London: Routledge.

Oloka-Onyango J. (2000) "New Wine or New Bottles? Movement Politics and One-Partyism In Uganda" in Oloka-Onyango, J. and Mugaju, J. *No-Party Democracy In Uganda: Myths and Realities.* Kampala: Fountain Publishers.

Orwell, G. (1952) *Nineteen Eighty-Four.* Harmondsworth, Middlesex: Penguin

Orwell, G. (1972) *Animal Farm* London: Heinemann Educational

Postman, A. (1985) *Amusing Ourselves to Death: Public Discourse In the Age of Show Business.* New York, NY: Penguin.

Stephens, M. (1997) *A History of the News* Orlando, Fl: Harcout Brace & Company.

Sunday Vision (2003) *Gae, Abby Have Sex on Live TV* June 29, 2003 pp 1. Kampala: The New Vision Printing & Publishing Co.

The Daily Telegraph (2001) "Yes, These Shows are Exploitative, Says Mr Big Brother: July 19, 2001 pp.1. http://www.telegraph.co.uk/news/2001/07/19. Accessed on Aug. 25, 2003

The Monitor (2003) "Millions Watch Big Brother Africa" May 28, 2003 pp 1. Kampala: Nation Media Group.

The Monitor (2003) "Out & About" Aug. 30, 2003 pp 17. Kampala: Nation Media Group.

The New Vision (2003) "Have You Heard?" Aug. 30, 2003 pp. 11. Kampala: The New Vision Printing and Publishing Co.

The Population Secretariat (1999) *Population Levels, Trends & Characteristics.* Ministry of Finance Kampala: Uganda Printing and Publishing Corporation.

The United Nations Development Programme (2003) *Human Development Index 2003 Country Report, Uganda.* New York, NY: UNDP.

Yankelovich, D. (1991) *Coming to Public Judgement: Making Democracy Work in a Complex World.* Syracuse, NY: Syracuse University Press.

4

The Challenges of Reporting the Northern Uganda Armed Conflict

John Muto-Ono p'Lajur

Introduction

In their analysis of newspaper coverage of military operations in northern Uganda from January 2002 to 2003, the Acholi Religious Leaders Peace Initiative (ARLPI), commissioned a report entitled "War of Words".

Justice Resource, a Kampala-based consultancy firm working on issues of human rights, conflict and access to justice, produced the report. The foreword of the document partly states:

> When newspapers report – sometimes with some amount of rejoicing – that so many rebels have been killed over a certain period of time and one finds later on that a good number of them were in fact abducted children [should they escape, they will be referred to not as 'rebels' but as 'rescued abductees' it means that the truth is not being honoured, and when this is the case, it becomes difficult to build a real 'shalom', (Psalm 85), a sustainable peace of right relationship among human beings."

It is an analysis of the Uganda newspapers' coverage of military operations in northern Uganda from January 2002 to February 2003.

In conflict situations, the media should ideally be a forum for bridging the gap between warring parties (parties in conflict). It should provide a channel of communication through which the conflicting parties can dialogue so as to reach a consensus.

The media is also a 'voice for the voiceless', which should give direction of movement for the general good of the society.

It is wrong for media practitioners to promote and advance views which escalate, rather than de-escalate, conflict.

For example, it is wrong for a sub-editor to keep asking the question, "How many rebels are killed?"

It is also wrong for a reporter to say "For me I don't believe (in peace talks)" or to say "These people should just be killed."

Such sub-editors and reporters should know they are like fans watching a football match from the pavilion. "You are a fan outside the arena; not a player entertaining spectators."

Such journalists, if given a chance, usually kill the accused even before the judge pronounces the death penalty.

Unlike in a football game where the players are actually sweating it out in the field, a journalist (reporter) can actually enjoy the game of reporting and yet not allow himself to be drawn into the field in the same way spectators are from the pavilion.

At times they can be like the referee who also runs around in the same field as the players, although he may not be able to enjoy, or to laugh as much as the fans outside the arena.

Journalists (reporters) should not behave like those fans who turn around and throw stones and bottles at the players when the side which they support loses. They do not join in the celebrations of the victorious team either.

The greatest challenge of reporting the conflict in northern Uganda, and indeed any other conflict area in the whole world, is for the journalist to use all communication channels to the maximum. In this way all the issues would be brought out into the open so that solutions could be found to such conflicts.

What is Communication?

The Oxford Advanced Learner's Dictionary of Current English defines communication as a noun from the verb 'to communicate'.
There are four different definitions of the infinitive 'to communicate'.

The first meaning is to make something known. An example of this is: "*Miguel Street* communicates the disillusionment of the people of Port of Spain."

It also means to pass something on, to transmit something. That is why some diseases are known as communicable diseases, diseases that can be passed on.

The second meaning is to exchange information, news, ideas, etc. with somebody.

It also means to make one's ideas, feelings, emotions, etc. clear to others. For example, when you say "I love you very much."

The third meaning of the word 'communicate' is to have a good relationship because of shared feelings and understanding:

"Something must be wrong with our marriage – we don't seem to communicate anymore."

The fourth meaning of the same word is to be connected with. An example of this is communicating rooms, i.e. rooms with connecting doors like the coaches of a train.

Communication is the action or process of communicating. An example is a disease or message. Means of communication include roads, railways, telephone lines between places, radios, televisions, etc.

A communication cord passes along the length of a train. One is able to move from one coach to another while the train is moving as a result.

Lack of communication, dialogue and inadequate use of the media are some of the major factors that are detrimental to any peace building or conflict resolution.

Face-to-face communication, when one is able to see the gestures and facial expressions on the other's face, can be very useful in building rapport and in conflict transformation.

Even nature communicates with us, forcing us to react accordingly. When one is faced with dusty conditions one becomes wise by covering one's face like 'Arab' women do.

We react to communications positively when our reactions do not promote conflict. The reverse is true when we react to communication negatively.

Communication can be facilitated through maximum use of the different media available, and modern information technology (IT).

What is Conflict?

The dictionary defines conflict either as a noun or as a verb.

When used as a noun, conflict is schism - a serious state of disagreement. It is a struggle, a fight.

Conflict is a serious difference of opinion aspiration. It is an argument between opposing groups or opposing ideas or principles.

When used as a verb, conflict refers to being very different from something, being in opposition, clashing.

We can for instance say, "Their account of events conflict with ours."

Conflict is 'a necessary evil' and exists in all human beings. Conflict is part of our existence. Conflict is not necessarily a bad thing.

It is intra-personal when we face the choice between this and that alternative in our lives.

We need conflict in order to develop because after conflict, change takes place. Change can be for the better or for the worse, depending on how it is perceived.

Conflict is never a static phenomenon. It is expressive, dynamic and dialectical. Conflict is constantly changed by ongoing human interaction, and it continuously changes the very people who give it life and the social environment in which it is born, evolves and perhaps ends.

> The paradox of conflict is that it is both the force that can tear relationships apart and it is the force which binds them together. This dual nature of conflict makes it an important concept to study and understand. Conflict can be managed negatively through avoidance at one extreme and the use or threat of force at the other. Alternatively, conflict can be managed positively through negotiations, joint problem solving and consensus building. These options help build and sustain constructive bilateral and multi-lateral relations. Some of our responses to conflict are constructive, but others can escalate conflict and raise the level of danger. What can start to change destructive responses to conflict is learning to assess the total impact of negative responses and acquiring confidence in using tools and techniques of professional peacemakers.

> Differences in viewpoint are inevitable and often enriching. When people study a problem together, they often assume that with the same facts at everyone's disposal, they will all agree on a single analysis. This is not so. Unanimity is even more unlikely when in addition to these 'natural' differences, there are those brought about by a range of other dimensions: status, power, wealth, age, the role assigned to our gender, belonging to a specific social group, and so on.

> We consider that these indicators of position in society often mean that the people want different things from the same situation: sometimes these goals clash, or are incompatible. It is then that we have a conflict.

Differences in perspectives and goals are sometimes seen as a problem that will only be resolved when we have the same intentions, or when one view wins over the others.

Alternatively, conflicts can be seen as a resource, leading to a wider understanding of a problem, and an improvement to the present situation."

What is Peace?

There is sometimes a difference between "negative peace" and "positive peace". Negative peace refers to the absence of violence. It is negative because something undesirable stopped happening.

Positive peace is filled with positive content such as restoration of relationships, creation of social systems that serve the needs of the whole populations and the constructive resolution of conflict.

Peace does not mean total absence of any conflict. It means the absence of violence in all its forms and the unfolding of conflict in a constructive way. Peace therefore exists where people are interacting non-violently and are managing their conflicts positively – with respectful attention to the legitimate needs and interests of all concerned.

Reconciliation becomes necessary when negative conflict had occurs and relationships are damaged. Reconciliation is important in situations of high interdependence where a complete physical or emotional barrier between parties in conflict cannot be maintained. Reconciliation refers to the restoration of relationships to a level where co-operation and trust becomes possible again.

Lederach (1995) states that reconciliation deals with three specific paradoxes:

- Reconciliation promotes an encounter between the open expression of the painful past and the search for the articulation of the long-term interdependent future.

- Reconciliation provides a place for truth and mercy to meet, where concern for exposing what happened and letting go in favour of a renewed relationship are validated and embraced.

- Reconciliation recognises the need to give time and place to justice and peace, where redressing the wrong is held together with the vision of a common, connected future.

Functions of Conflict

Some of the positive aspects of conflict as noted by Coser (1956) are:
1. Conflicts help establish our identity and independence.
2. Intensity of conflict demonstrates the closeness and importance of relationships.
3. Conflict can build new relationships.
4. Conflict can create coalitions.
5. Conflict serves as a safety-valve mechanism, which helps to sustain relationships.
6. Conflict helps parties assess each other's power and can work to redistribute power in a system of conflict.
7. Conflict establishes and maintains group identities.
8. Conflicts enhance group cohesion through issue and belief clarification.
9. Conflict creates or modifies rules, norms, laws and institutions.

Conflict Resolution Terms

Co-operative problem-solving; negotiation; mediation; facilitation; and arbitration.

Conflicts at play in Northern Uganda

There are different types and forms of conflict at play in northern Uganda, some of which are salient conflicts:

> Faced with hostilities from Sudan People's Liberation Army (SPLA) from the Sudan and the National resistance Army (NRA) from Uganda, the refugees became desperate and took up arms in self-defence of their rights and to ensure their survival (*Goodwill mission report to the President and the people of Uganda*, 1987).

Veteran politician Tiberio Okeny-Atwoma led a 5-man mission that spent 42 days in the Uganda People's Democratic Army (UPDA) camp and documented the causes of the war in northern Uganda as basic and immediate.

The UPDA gave six reasons for fighting the NRM/A government

a. Violation of the Nairobi Peace Accord by NRM/A.

b. Invasion of Uganda by refugees from Rwanda in flagrant violation of the Geneva Convention of 1951.

c. Diabolical and wanton killings of innocent Ugandans, particularly in Gulu and Kitgum districts.

d. Violation of human rights in Uganda by NRM/A.

e. Introduction of communistic ideology and practices in Uganda by NRM/A.

f. Dictatorship and discrimination in Uganda by NRM/A.

The immediate causes as documented by the mission are:

a. Destruction of Magwi refugee camp in the Sudan by SPLA where many Ugandans lost their lives and property forcing them to flee back into Uganda and meeting with discouragement and hostility by NRM/A at home.

b. Violation of the human rights of Ugandans who returned from the Sudan by NRM in spite of the government's call and assurances. In May 1986, the NRA began harassing and tormenting innocent returnees and peasants in Acholi. The NRA did this during the government exercise of collecting guns from the people by tying them in the inhuman style commonly referred to as "kandoya".

c. Discriminatory dismissal of officers and men serving in the Uganda Police and Prison forces and other officials in public institutions.

Background to the Conflicts in Northern Uganda

We do not have to go back to the colonial period in order to understand the background of the conflicts in Northern Uganda.

We do not even need to know how those who went into exile in Tanzania were in conflict with one another because their ethnicity or status in society gave birth to later liberation movements such as FRONASA, Force Obote Back Again (FOBA) or WNBF. Such conflicts laid the foundation for the mutual mistrust, which developed between the different regions and tribes.

Many Acholi were burnt to death on Kampala streets using motor-vehicle tyres because they were *'anyanya'* (poison). This was the name adopted by the first rebels in southern Sudan in 1955. The NRA used it to generate hatred against the Acholi whom they accused of killing people in Luwero Triangle.

The rebellion in Acholi was basically an extension of the one which began in Luwero Triangle on 6th February 1981 and which was launched by incumbent President Yoweri Museveni, and 26 others. That conflict saw the exit of two presidents – Dr. Apollo Milton Obote, whose second rule lasted from December 1980 to 27th July 1985, and General Tito Okello Lutwa who ruled Uganda from 27th July 1985 to 25th January 1986.

Gen. Okello Lutwa invited the NRA out of the bush when he overthrew Obote and went ahead to commission Salim Saleh to represent the rebels in government. The marriage between the two was short-lived. War continued until negotiations were held and later the Nairobi Peace Agreement was signed before President Daniel Arap Moi of Kenya. Many people called it "peace jokes". The NRA eventually overthrew Tito Okello.

Many of the former UNLA soldiers tried to regroup inside southern Sudan in order to reclaim state power, and launched their first attack on Bibia NRA barracks along the border with Sudan on 16th August 1986. This time the struggle was not national like the one against Amin, which was decided upon at Moshi, Tanzania in 1978.

There was the National Union for the Liberation of Uganda (NALU) led by Amon Bazira (RIP) in western Uganda and Force Obote Back Again (FOBA) led by individuals such as Hon. Aggrey Awori in eastern Uganda. There was also Uganda People's Army (UPA) in the Teso and Lango sub-region where leaders like Musa Ecwero and Max Omeda were very active. Others such as Peter Otai are still in exile.

Two rebellions emerged in West Nile alone, namely the West Nile Bank Front (WNBF), and the Uganda National Rescue Front (UNRF) led by prominent individuals such as Brig. Moses Ali (now Lt. Gen.) and Col. Juma Oris (RIP) respectively.

Former UNLA soldiers from the Acholi sub-region were not in agreement regarding what to do with the change of regime in Kampala. Many decided to surrender and co-operate with the new leadership. With the help of elders like Wilson Lutara, Hon. James Obol-Ochola (RIP), Levy Arweny and Tiberio Okeny-Atwoma, some of these former soldiers collected the guns they had escaped with, surrendered and handed them over to the government. They went on to settle into civilian life.

However, some of them from Koch Goma, Alero, Anaka and Purongo sub-counties, and Nwoya county in Gulu, refused to surrender their guns to elders. They wanted these guns for poaching in the nearby Murchison Falls National Game Park.

Another group decided to go into exile in neighbouring southern Sudan and to register as refugees there. People such as Charles Alai found themselves leaders of this group. They registered themselves as refugees with the United Nations High Commissioner for Refugees (UNHCR).

However, some of them people escaped with their guns, which had been hidden away from either Ugandan or Sudanese leaders.

Some took advantage of the upheaval to seek political asylum. Some of these were not persecuted, but went out in search of greener pastures. Some of them, such as Olara-Otunu (then Minister of Foreign Affairs in the Okello junta), who played a central role in the Nairobi peace talks had every reason to fear, and therefore sought asylum. Olara-Otunu was even stripped of his Ugandan citizenship.

The NRM/A leadership dealt with these rebellions one by one and signed peace agreements with them separately before integrating their fighting forces into the NRA. The government signed peace accords with only sections of these movements and most of the individuals involved were the young Turks.

For instance, Moses Ali left Col. Juma Oris in the UNRF I while Col. Angelo Okello Kent and Charles Alai left Brig. Odong-Latek and Eric Otema-Allimadi in the UPDM/A.

What Went Wrong?

President Museveni addressed NRA soldiers at the Karuma bridge in April 1986 before they crossed into northern Uganda. People advance different reasons as to why it took so long for the new regime to liberate northern Uganda.

One group say some Ugandans wanted the NRM/A to cut-off Acholiland from the rest of Uganda. The delay to liberate Acholiland was seen as punishment for their role in the war in Luwero. Others accused the Acholi of plundering Lira town and also of overthrowing the Obote II regime.

Another group, especially the elite, believed that whereas the NRA crossed Karuma into the north during the liberation of the country, the NRM remained behind.

The NRM chose to work with new and young leadership, most of whom had campaigned for President Museveni's party, the Uganda Patriotic Movement (UPM) in the run-up to the 1980 general election.

The leaders had little contact with the very people they should lead. Many people looked at them as instruments of oppression instead. The leaders began to look at the people as enemies of the new regime who should either be coerced into supporting the new regime or be alienated altogether.

This is contrary to the kind of politics in Buganda where even Kabaka Ronald Mutebi was drawn into supporting NRM. Other Baganda leaders such as the late Prof. Yusuf Lule and Dr Samson Kisekka were instrumental in creating harmony between the regime and the Baganda.

The first group of NRA to cross into Acholi were very friendly. Some of them who were in the UNLA but joined the NRA after Kampala fell would visit the villages of their former colleagues who had opted to resettle in civilian life. There was merrymaking during which the former soldier would entertain NRA soldiers. There was peace.

However, things changed around June 1986 when this group was replaced by another group of NRA soldiers. These were former FEDEMU soldiers who came to Acholiland to 'avenge' all the atrocities committed in Luwero Triangle by UNLA soldiers. They did not look at UNLA as a national army with all tribes in it. To them UNLA was Acholi and every Acholi was a UNLA soldier. They introduced indiscipline within NRA.

Some of these soldiers began to undress and rape women. They claimed that the UNLA soldiers who were in the Luwero Triangle had looted the *gomesis* the women in Acholi wore.

The most memorable of such atrocities were committed in Namokora sub-county, Chua county in Kitgum, the birthplace of former President Gen. Tito Okello-Lutwa.

In Soroti, the roasting of innocent civilians in a railway wagon was simply a caricature extension of what had happened in Namokora. They also practised sodomy.

The second group of NRA soldiers included elements with business interests. Many of them joined the NRA during the Luwero bush war as fugitives from the law because they were robbers, petty thieves and other kinds of outlaws. The NRA welcomed these people into their ranks but did very little to rehabilitate them.

When they crossed into Acholi, they looted propety such as motor vehicles, milling machines, sewing machines. They also dismantled fencing poles and de-roofed the houses of private citizens as well as buildings belonging to government institutions such as ranches. They even turned school desks into firewood.

Data or Information Conflict

First of all, the value of information today is usually measured in terms of the interest generated by consumers. Information is treated as a commodity like any other commodity that must be sold. No matter how truthful a piece of information, may be, if it does not spark any interest in the public it will lack economic value.

The discovery that information is marketable and that it may generate great financial gain has attracted a lot of investment. Businessmen who seek profit have replaced selfless truth-seekers. Ever since this concept was understood, information has stopped being measured by its authenticity, rather it is measured according to the law of the marketplace: how to achieve maximum profit and maintain this situation of privilege in the face of competition from other media enterprises. This may account for the fact that when conflict arises in different parts of the world, the media usually mention a selected few or maybe only one – the one that will attract what Polish journalist Richard Kapuscinski once called the big herd" (*War of Words* pp v – vi).

There is lack of information, concealment of information, propaganda and misinformation, between the warring parties and the affected community. In order to suppress information, the government downplays any negative image and is not interested in exposing what is going on in the war zone. It is particularly concerned with its international image, that is, of being progressive, democratic, a respecter of human rights and such other good qualities.

The government is also concerned with keeping the morale of the army high in order to encourage them to fight on. When soldiers lose morale, they lose in interest fighting the rebels and therefore may lose the war. They may not want to expose the soldiers to the truth about casualties.

Their spokesmen resort to a kind of propaganda instead of telling the truth about the state of affairs on the battle front.

When in 1996 the Lord's Resistance Army (LRA) struck the outskirts of Kitgum town, the *New Vision* and the *Monitor* reporters were there to witness what had happened. When the stories eventually appeared in the two dailies, the leadership in Kitgum in the persons of the Resident District Commissioner (RDC) and the Chairman Local Council V threatened to mobilise villagers to spear to death any journalist who dared to report about rebel atrocities in Kitgum. Their argument was that the journalists would scare away investors interested in the district.

The then Minister of State for Pacification in Northern Uganda, Mrs Betty Bigombe, had to intervene and defuse the tension between journalists and the local leaders in Kitgum.

To date, journalists do not cover events in Kitgum extennsively as they do in Gulu.

The army leadership was not comfortable after they involved some members of the community mutilating the dead body of a notorious LRA rebel called "Beba Beba" and lynching some suspected LRA rebels and collaborators in a stage-managed incident of mob justice in front of the Gulu main market on the Moroto road in 1996. The press covered that episode extensively. To date, the army has not repeated the mistake bringing rebel suspects to be lynched by "angry civilians".

The Kandida Lakony (RIP) saga of 11th May 1999 and the court case against her and *The Monitor* over the published photo in addition to the closure of *The Monitor* head office on the night of 15th October 2002 are a few examples to illustrate my point.

On the other hand, the LRA has never encouraged the use of the media in the same way other rebel movements the world over would. The only explanation is that the LRA commits atrocities to such unprecedented levels that exposing such atrocities haunts them.

The LRA reaction to the use of information in order to propagate their cause is contrary to what the National Resistance Army/Movement (NRA/M) did when they invited William Pike (now *The New Vision* editor-in-chief) to the bush in the Luwero Triangle to help them produce the audiovisual documentary *"The Horrors of Kapeeka"*.

That film helped to build the international image of the NRA/M, as a pro-people's army/movement. In that way the NRA/M succeeded in discrediting Obote II government both nationally and internationally.

The Sudan government, which is the main backer and supporter of the LRA, has a similar policy regarding the war in southern Sudan, which has been going on since 1955.

The Khartoum government strongly remonstrated when the Archbishop of Canterbury, Dr William Carey, paid a pastoral visit to southern Sudan. They feared that the archbishop's entourage, which usually includes members of the media, would expose what was actually going on in southern Sudan.

Infrastructures such as human settlements and roads along the common border between Sudan and Uganda have been destroyed by the prolonged war inside Sudan. A large chunk of no-man's land exists between the Sudan and most of its neighbours:

Relationship Conflict

Bad relationships occur as a result of poor communication and unfriendly social and cultural interactions or relationships. Communication is equal to information plus understanding. Where any component is lacking, there are bound to be problems in such as relationship.

Acholi used to be a cosmopolitan land with different tribes living in harmony until the 25th January 1971 coup by dictator Idi Amin Dada (RIP). The Madi, Lugbara, Nubians, Banyoro, Banyankole (commonly called Balalu), Langi and Alur had integrated fully into the community.

Some of these people acquired land and assets and they hold important positions in Acholiland. Few people know that "Lord" Andrew Adimola, who is a highly respected and retired politician in Acholi, is a descendant of a family whose real ancestors came from Nebbi district.

During the struggle to liberate Uganda from Idi Amin, President Yoweri Museveni and Akena p'Ojok (an Acholi now living in exile) worked together in Acholi as others, such as leaders opposed to Idi Amin were mobilising and recruiting youths and taking them to Tanzania through southern Sudan in a mission which was commonly referred in Acholi as "*yango lyec*", meaning skinning the elephant. One of the people involved in these activities was Milton Obote. That journey took the youths through Owiny-ki-Bul via Port Sudan in Sudan then on to Dar-es-Salaam in Tanzania via the Red Sea.

Museveni and Akena p'Ojok established training camps in Pupwonya parish in Attiak and in Awere sub-county in Gulu district. Some of the people trained by the two in Pupwonya are still alive.

Amos Obwona (RIP) and John Labeja (RIP) were the first heroes in Ugandan history to be executed by firing squad by the Amin regime in Kampala on 10th February 1973 after they were betrayed by a section of the Acholi community. A monument built in memory of them, which was unveiled by former President Godfrey Binasia on 3rd November 1979 at Boma Ground in Gulu municipality, stands just a few metres away from where they were executed.

The survivors have revealed that the two heroes were betrayed for various reasons, including religious and political differences.

Relationships between the Acholi and the settlers began to deteriorate in 1971 when soldiers of the Amin regime began killing members of the Acholi elite and those who were in the forces.

When Amin was overthrown on 11th April 1979, those who had associated themselves with his regime fled Acholi for fear of revenge.

One Muslim called Jakariya Juma (RIP) took refuge in my bedroom for three days until after the mayhem of revenge was over.

The Uganda militia, which was composed mostly by the Acholi and Langi, extended the same kind of revenge to Yumbe in 1980 in an effort to quell a possible rebellion against the UNLA/F government.

Tension later flared up between the Acholi and the Langi in July 1985 when a section of the UNLA led by its Commander General Tito Okello-Lutwa (R.I.P) overthrew the Milton Obote II regime on 27th July 1985.

The Langi accused one particular Acholi commander, Maj. Stephen Odyek alias Ojukwu, of indiscriminate killings in the Lango sub-region and plundering Lira municipality.

The Balalu (employed in Acholi as cattle keepers and whose wages were in the form of milk) fled Acholi after the NRA/M took over power. Many Acholi believe that this group of herdsmen came as an advance team of NRA intelligence to spy on Acholi cattle for eventual rustling when they (NRA) take over. Many Balalu led NRA soldiers in looting in Acholi villages.

Resource or Structural Conflicts

Resource conflicts are caused by unequal distribution of resources, power and the unjust social systems. A look at Uganda's history can provide an important insight in this respect.

The colonial masters thought the Acholi were only good for the armed forces, the Lugbara from West Nile were suited to farm work, the Indians were traders while the Baganda were good as civil servants and agents of the colonial masters.

During the NRA struggle (6th February 1981 to 26th January 1986) in Luwero Triangle, Ugandans began to hear expressions like *"ufupi sio ugonyjwa"*, *the Kiswahili expression* meaning "to be short does not mean you are sick." If the British had continued to rule Uganda to date, no Bakonjo would have been recruited into the Ugandan army because very few Bakonjo would stand above five feet.

The 18-year-old war in northern Uganda has also increased socio-economic disparity between the region and other parts of the country. There are few *mabati* (iron sheet roofed) houses north of the Karuma bridge. Conversely, there are few grass-thatched huts after Masaka as one goes onwards to Mbarara and beyond.

Many foreign missions to Uganda frequently issue advisories to their nationals against travelling to northern Uganda. There are more NGOs operating in Mpigi alone than in the entire northern Uganda.

Value Conflicts

Value conflict occurs as a result of different levels of understanding of issues, ideological or philosophical thinking, different cultures and lifestyles.

We can safely say that the war in northern Uganda is an extension of the one which began in Luwero Triangle on the 6th February 1981. The defeated UNLA soldiers, who were mostly from northern Uganda, resisted the change because they valued being in the army more than being in any other job.

The victorious (NRA/M) also preached hatred against the vanquished as they moved northwards. Many people witnessed mob justice meted out to innocent *anyanya* by burning them to death using car tyres immediately Kampala fell on 26th January 1986.

The patriotic military song *'Sirina dollar, anyanya'* (a Luganda song meaning 'the northerners have no dollar' was very popular.

Value conflict is most difficult to stamp out because it occurs in our minds; it is related to what we think and believe. We need time to understand, to begin to appreciate others with divergent views, to accommodate others and try to live in diversity.

No two people, even if they are identical twins, can act the same way, believe and value the same thing. Being different makes it possible for us to have contrasts.

Artists and musicians know this. They can make perfect harmony using contrasts. We hear this in songs or hang it on our walls in the form of beautiful pictures. Music and pictures blend contrasts and make it beautiful and admirable.

Interest Conflicts

This conflict revolves around either real or imaginary competition over interests. You have heard philosophical lines of thinking such as; 'the end justifies the means' or 'the means justify the end'.

Many Ugandans know that the Owen Falls Dam in Jinja was built following a treaty between the British and the Egyptians, that the Egyptians have a permanent commission established by the same treaty to monitor the levels of the River Nile waters for a period of one hundred years, and that they have an interest in any project or investment on the river which may interfere with the level of the Nile water that flows through the country into the Mediterranean Sea. This is an example of interest conflicts.

Another example is what happened when both Milton Obote and Yoweri Museveni were in exile in Tanzania. Milton Obote established "Kikoosi Maalum" under Tito Okello Lutwa and Museveni established the Front for National Salvation (FRONASA) to fight Idi Amin.

Many people are convinced that the war on Iraq was more related 'interests' than what the Americans would like the world to believe.

Sometimes conflicts of interest prevent us from launching a common front against an enemy and divert our resources.

Conflict and Violence

Conflict is different from violence but it can lead to violence and destruction if it is badly perceived and mismanaged. Conflict can lead to violence if it is perceived as a FIGHT. Parties to the conflict must not blame each other and begin to think that the other party created the conflict. Conflict can also lead to aggression if it is conceived as a 'MEANS TO AN END'. Conflict can lead to constructive development if it is perceived as a 'PROBLEM TO BE SOLVED'.

Ugandans were united in Moshi, Tanzania in 1978 in forming the Uganda National Liberation Front/Army (UNLF/A) with the common objective of overthrowing Idi Amin. They would not have succeeded if each fighting group had begun to fight the others in order to gain control in Uganda after overthrowing Amin.

Conflict should therefore be perceived and interpreted in as many ways as there are different individuals and cultures.

Conflict and Peace

Where conflict exists, peace disappears. Peace is harmony. It is living and having plenty. Peace is co-existence with our surroundings and our environment. Peace is freedom. It is freedom from disorder within a country, with citizens living according to the law. Peace is freedom from anxiety or troubling thoughts. It is peace of mind – freedom from unwanted noise or activity. It is calmness.

We cannot say that Ugandans are living in peace. There is only partial peace. The people in some parts of the country are developing at commendable rate and have not heard a single gunshot or witnessed killings in many years.

But the people of northern Uganda have been in tears, singing dirges for the last eighteen years. Probably, other parts of the country are just beginning to feel the pinch of this rebellion; coffins bearing fallen sons from this senseless war are being ferried to different parts of the country.

Those living in peaceful environments should not be deceived that all is peaceful. Remember the story of the 'Lions of Tsavo' when the Indians were constructing the Uganda Railway. The man who slept in the safest corner thought the lions were not his problem, but that of the one who slept by the door of the wagon. At the end, many Indians were eaten by the lions.

Soldiers and Conflict

Every recruit in a military training camp is taught *'Usalama ya silaa'*. This is a Kiswahili phrase, meaning humbling oneself before the gun.

They are taught how to adore and respect the gun because it is one's 'mother and father.'

Soldiers are taught that the muzzle of the gun must always point towards the 'enemy position'. The muzzle must never point at the holder or at friendly forces.

'Usalama ya silaa' also helps the soldier to protect himself against any possible negligence. One has to check the safety of the gun before it changes hands. The one who gives out a gun makes sure that there is no bullet in the chambers before handing it over. The one who receives the gun must ensure that it is safe to hold it.

The War (Conflict) Theatre

The wars (read conflicts) in northern Uganda cover Nebbi, Arua, Yumbe, Moyo, Adjumani, Gulu, Kitgum, Pader, Lira, Apac, Kotido, Moroto, Nakapiripirit, Kaberamaido, Soroti, Kumi, Katakwi, Kapchorwa and Mbale districts. Some of these conflicts such as those involving UPA, WNBF, UNRF (I), UNRF (II), UPDA and HSM have been resolved.

The only two persisting conflicts are cattle rustling and the LRA rebellion. Rustling occurs mostly in Moroto, Kotido, Nakapiripirit, Kapchorwa, Mbale, Katakwi, Soroti, Kumi, Lira and Pader districts. Southern Sudan and eastern Kenya are also affected by rustling.

The LRA rebels operate mostly in Kitgum, Pader and Gulu districts of the Acholi sub-region. They have also extended their operations into neighbouring Apac, Lira, Adjumani, Soroti, Kumi and Kaberamaido Katakwi districts. They also have a base in Southern Sudan.

The effect of the LRA war is also felt in Masindi and Nebbi districts owing to the influx of internal refuges there. Displaced people from Acholi are developing Byeyaale and Karuma trading centres in Kibanda county in Masindi district.

President Yoweri Museveni has always blamed the difficult terrain in the region in addition to inadequate funding to the army for the delays in ending the conflict militarily.

There is a vast no-man's land along the common border with Sudan, which is inhabited. The rebels can hide there for as long as they want. There are neither human beings nor infrastructure to facilitate monitoring of rebel movements.

When one UPDF went inside the Sudan during "Operation Iron Fist" (IOF), some of them had to buy goats at sixty thousand and chickens at eighteen thousand Ugandan shillings each because there was a shortage of them.

Rivers such as Aswa, Pager, Aringa, and Agago are difficult to cross, while transporting the armoured conventional weapons preferred by the UPDF. On the other hand, the rebels can cross these rivers using ropes, while the UPDF have to get round this problem by using security roads, most of which are still under construction.

Conventional Warfare

Conventional warfare has marked front lines for the warring parties. The gap between the two is called a 'no man's land'. Crossing this point is dangerous, as you will be treated as a spy by the side that catches you.

Journalists only report from the side on which the war gets them except on rare occasions.

In northern Uganda, the UPDF do not allow journalists to go to rebel camps even though opportunities to do so can be available. Only three local journalists have ever reached rebel camps since the war began in 1986. Caroline Lamwaka did so during the Uganda People's Democratic Army (UPDA) rebellion before the signing of the 3rd June 1988 agreement. Billy O'Kademaeri was at an LRA camp during peace talks together with Betty Bigombe in 1994, and so was Nahaman Ojwee in 2001 together with Gulu Local Council V Chairman, Lt Col. Walter Ochora-Odoch at Awor-Nyim in Bungatira sub-county.

There is no front line in the UPDF-LRA war, as would exist in a conventional one. The only conventional warfare we witnessed was when the Tanzanians and Ugandan exiles were liberating Uganda from Idi Amin in 1978-1979 and when the UNLA soldiers were retreating northwards after the fall of Kampala to the NRA in January 1986.

When President Yoweri Museveni asked the LRA to assemble in specific places either inside Sudan or within Uganda in August 2002 and again during the abortive ceasefire of 2003, he was trying to create a kind of conventional front which would have allowed the LRA easy access to basic supplies like food and medicine from the international community.

The rebels feared that that those offers were ploys to get them to assemble in one position so as to enable the UPDF to bomb them. They have never accepted the proposition for a de-militarised zone at Koyo-Lalogi and Wiipolo villages in Lapul sub-county, Aruu county in Pader district to allow the LRA so meet contacts for dialogue.

Insurgency/Guerrilla Warfare

This is the situation pertaining in northern Uganda. The warring parties can confront one another anywhere and at any time. This can be in the middle of a crowded market. This has a great impact on the unarmed civilians because one cannot predict the direction events would take.

Imagine that as Billie O'Kadermeri was busy documenting the Bigombe-Kony meeting where only the LRA soldiers had guns, fighting erupted all of a sudden. Some of us would urinate on our trousers. Journalists such as Emmy Allio (*New Vision*) and Ono Colombus (Simba FM) who survived crossfires as they were travelling along the roads are still alive to tell their stories. Again, Dennis Ojwee (*The New Vision*) and Oketch Bitek (*The Monitor*) have tales to tell about the crashing in a battle area of a helicopter they were travelling in.

Election Period

This is a situation characterised by political manoeuvre, which usually degenerates into violent conflicts and deaths. The late Higenyi was a victim of political violence in 2001. Whereas it is easy to avoid taking sides in open armed conflicts, journalists are often partisan when it comes to politics during election time. Expressions like 'he who pays the piper calls the tune' are too common in our newsrooms. Only ethics and values can resolve this dilemma.

This document aims to support journalists on a new and rewarding career path, where their unique contribution to problem-solving is recognised and embraced. This approach enhances the consumers' interest in media reporting and analysis.

Cynicism and disenchantment with the media can be overcome using a conflict-resolving approach. The rapidity of political, social and environmental change leaves societies in massive and unresolved conflict, while at hand is the under-utilised resource of the media, whose help is too seldom sought. The media may need to go beyond fact-delivery and find the conflict-resolving talent.

Attribution

Three groups – the LRA rebels, the UPDF (including Home Guards and Local Defence Units) and outlaws commonly referred to as *'bookec'*, (*they do not want to eat green vegetables because they are bitter*) commit atrocities.

Frequently, journalists attribute every bad act to the LRA and give credit to the UPDF for all good acts. This is bad because we are not presenting facts as they are because of certain assumptions. The UPDF are not able to discipline some of their erring officers because we give false reports.

Respect of Front Lines

It is dangerous to try to cross front lines and to report from the other side of the conflict. No story is worth one's life. One must live to tell that story. But, with modern communication skills, the front line should not prevent a journalist from getting access to the other side.

It is unfortunate that the LRA is such a closed organisation that it does not want publicity through the press or media. Otherwise we would be quoting many of the LRA statements alongside the UPDF ones.

Statistics/Figures

Many journalists are guilty of misrepresenting facts by publishing wrong figures. We should realise that sources that give us figures have special interests.

The World Food Programme (WFP), for example, would like to give horrifying photographs from some famine-stricken African village and say one million people are starving in Southern Sudan so as to attract funds.

The UPDF would like to highlight successes against the LRA while downplaying their losses. When the UPDF refused to admit that a Major (name withheld) was killed in the north, yet the major's family were informed about the death, two different stories by two different reporters converged at a newsroom; and the readers had a field day.

If we go by the statistics in press reports, the number of LRA rebels killed during the insurgency could be more than the number who actually joined the rebellion.

Taking Sides in the Conflict

The journalist must not be a party to the conflict. He/she should facilitate dialogue and communication between the parties to the conflict with the sole aim of resolving the conflict. By taking sides, the journalist would be escalating the conflict instead.

Clarifying Issues

The journalists must be scientific as far as facts are concerned; those relating to the players in the conflict, the positions and issues. Conflicts are dynamic, with issues, positions and facts changing from time to time. We are obliged, therefore, to be abreast with the changes taking place.

Choosing Words

For instance the riot between Muslims and Christians in Kaduna, Nigeria, which left over two hundred dead, is blamed on the press report which suggested that even prophet Mohammed would have approved of the beauty pageants which should have taken place in that city and that he would have even married one of the contestants. Editors are most guilty when they write sensational headlines with the selfish aim of selling their product.

Exploring Options

This is developed by all players and stakeholders, including journalists, as the whole picture is unfolding before them. Uganda is militarily fighting the LRA in the north, but it is also engaged in dialogue, negotiations and a diplomatic offensive against the same rebels. Sometimes this may involve engaging with issues to be discussed by the warring parties so as to reach a common position. Negotiations in Dar-es-Salaam (Tanzania) about Burundi, the one in Pretoria (South Africa) about the Democratic Republic of the Congo and the one in Machakos (Kenya) about the Sudan are classic examples.

Moving to the Positive

Ask questions like: 'What would it take to solve this problem?' 'What is it that you want?' 'What would make it better?' 'What would make you willing or change your position?' You should note that we are working to prevent violence and its visible and invisible effects such as deaths and hatred and the need to prevent the spirit of 'revenge'.

Appropriate Assertiveness

The journalists should expose the abuse of ethical standards and should steer protagonists towards the search for a solution. An attempt should be made to encourage them to say what is pertinent to them as individuals rather than hiding under the umbrella of a group. Personal attacks should not be encouraged or sensationalised. They should be helped to show the best, not the worst of themselves. People's real problems should be shown clearly and one should go beyond their fear of speaking out.

Empathy

> Reporting atrocities should be handled with care. Many of the combatants in this war are children who have been abducted against their wishes. The government should not be seen to rejoice in the death of these children. The use of language must be carefully considered for it influences public opinion. Words such as enemy, rebels, terrorists do not build trust or an environment for a peaceful reconciliation.

(Report of the Northern Dialogue for Peace workshop held at Gulu Primary Teachers College 8-9th May 2002.)

This is the ability to imagine and share another person's feelings, experiences, etc. You should avoid simplistic representations of the good/ bad, the right/wrong. Provide enough information and platform to create empathy for all sides. Where empathy breakdown is the cause of conflict, expose it. Labelling, stereotyping or prejudice need to be addressed.

Brown Envelopes

The saying that 'he who plays the piper calls the tune' should not apply to journalists who are working towards solving conflicts. Journalists should learn to reject the organisations that give them rides in Pajeros because such organisations may want to cover up some dirty schemes.

It can, however, be risky to take a ride in UPDF helicopter to a battlefield and still be able to report that the rebels outmanoeuvred the UPDF. Next time they will not transport you to the front line.

News Beats

A reporter in the northern Uganda war zone has a geographical beat rather than specialised reporting. He must deal with war, disaster, health, crime, courts, culture, religion, etc.

Tools of Trade

Basic tools of trade such as the pen, recorder and camera are a must. This helps the reporter in case of legal defence.

Radio Presenters' Dilemma

Gulu and Kitgum have developed a kind of relationship in which the LRA have been joining public debates 'on air' through phone-ins. Some presenters tremble upon hearing a rebel call and therefore risk messing up the smooth flow of the programme on air.

Notes

[1] Acholi Religious Leaders' Peace Initiatives
P.O. Box 104 Gulu
E-mail: arlpi@africaonline.co.ug
Web: w.w.w.acholipeace.org
Justice Resource
P.O. 226622, Kampala.
E-mail: justiceresources@yahoo.co.uk

[2] Institute of Customer Services Ltd.
P.O. 427200100, Nairobi,
Kenya.
E-mail. Icsconsultancy @yahoo.co.uk.

[3] (Working with Conflict – Skills and Strategy for Action on page 3/4 by Responding to Conflict-UK)

[4] Foreword to the Foundation for Human Rights Initiative's Regional workshop on the conflict in northern Uganda at Gulu district Council Hall on 6-9th July 1997.

[5] A report of the Global People's Forum held in Johannesburg, South Africa from 24th August to 3rd September 3rd 2002, entitled:
A Sustainable World is Possible on the topic: redistribution-page 11-12).

6   Working with Conflict, Coalition for Peace in Africa.
     E-mail: copa@actionsupport.co.za
7   Goodwill Mission report of 13th April 1987.
8   The Advanced Learner's Dictionary.

5

Conflict in Karamoja: Bridging the Information Gap through Human Rights-based Communication

Nathan Byamukama

We are not dealing with men and cowardly thieves who know that what they are doing is morally wrong and is not admired by society they live in. We are dealing with determined brave warriors who will stop at nothing to achieve their aim – The only force that they respect is that only superior to their own and the only authority, that which can defeat them... the aim should be to strike 'holy terror' among people and show them that the government has enough warriors to combat their own and that they can reach any part of the district if and when the need arises.[2]

Introduction

Most of the information and messages about Karamoja are combative ones. They are messages of conflict and war, power, conflicts and guns. The Karimojong might not be interested in having power over others. They actually prefer collaboration and co-operation to combative intentions. If well-informed and well communicated to, people can accept responsibility for their own omissions and commissions and make important decisions about their own lives, as long as the message is transmitted in a sustainable, consistent, honest and rights-conscious language.

This article seeks to show that Karamoja and the Karimojong in and outside the conflict do not only lack information but also that whatever information is available is communicated in a manner that is not human rights-based and a medium that is not accessible, thus causing no positive impact on the social, political and economic transformation of Karamoja.

The paper also seeks to establish the causal link between information and communication in and about Karamoja for purposes of causing any meaningful impact on that society. It is our submission that what is lacking in Karamoja is not the information but the problem lies in the way the information is communicated.

The article situates the Karamoja conflict and its lack of information within the general context of underdevelopment of the region and within the concept of development as a human right. It looks at information and communication as having a causal relationship. In human rights, the right to information is part of communication rights[2]. Information includes facts and data in any medium or form. It can also be any communication or representation of knowledge or something that can be recorded or communicated.

In communication, usually a message (information) is sent, received, interpreted and then probably sentback (feed back). However, the practice might not be as straightforward. If the end product of that information is to be used to transform society, it is essential that the medium, content and the timing of the information and communication together with the nature and character of the transmitters and recipients is seriously taken into consideration. This is because human beings, unlike machines, are unique and diverse creatures with diverse abilities and potential, and capable of digesting the messages among themselves and with others to discern the meaning and determine a course of action within themselves and with each other. In the case of Karamoja, the problem is not that there is no information, nor that there is no communication but the message is largely resisted because it does not, in the main, speak to the core of their human rights.

Human rights-based communication is a term derived from the general idea of a "human rights approach to development". This approach puts the protection and realisation of human rights at the centre of every development effort. The approach applies in conflict as well as stable situations. It uses established and accepted human rights standards as a common framework for assessing and guiding sustainable development initiatives. From this perspective, the ultimate goal of development is to guarantee human rights to all human beings of all walks of life. Progressively respecting, promoting and fulfilling human rights obligations is seen as the way to achieve development. A rights-based approach to development is both a vision and a tool of analysis devoid of any political biases and interests but guided by moral and legal standards that apply equally to all humanity.

As a vision, the rights-based approach (RBA) to development is a conceptual framework for the process of human development that is normatively based on the international human rights standards and operationally directed to promoting and protecting human rights. As a tool RBA integrates the norms, standards and principles of the international human rights system into the plans, policies and processes of development.

The norms, standards and principles are found in the abundant international human rights instruments/treaties and declarations in place. Uganda is a party to most of these instruments and is enjoined by its own ratification of these instruments to comply with the norms and standards through the Constitution of the Republic of Uganda and all other related laws. The underlying principles of the human rights-based approach include: express linkage to rights; equality and equity; accountability; empowerment; participation; non-discrimination and attention to the vulnerable groups.

Defining Human Rights-Based Approach to Information and Communication

The rights-based approach to information and communication deliberately and explicitly focuses on people with a view to ensure that they achieve minimum information and communication necessary for the enjoyment of the minimum conditions for living with dignity. It does so by exposing the root cause of lack of information and the vulnerability and marginalisation that it carries with it, with the aim of expanding the range of responses from the most vulnerable and the marginalised. A rights-based approach to communication empowers people to claim and exercise their rights to communicate and fulfil their responsibilities that come with these rights. The rights-based approach to communication recognises that poor and vulnerable people are also human beings entitled to human rights and invariably have inherent rights essential to livelihood, security and above all have the right to communicate. These rights are validated by international standards and laws.

In other words, the rights-based approach to communication seeks to empower all the people of all walks of life so that their voices are heard; identify those who have the duty to respect, promote and fulfil the right to communicate/information (duty bearers)[3] and those who need that right (right-holders)[4]; illuminate human rights issues so that they can specifically be targeted for implementation and communication, monitoring and evaluation; help in identifying institutional contributions in a given rights area for further implementation; is demand-driven and people can demand their rights (accountability); recognise the state's international human rights treaty obligations; ensure non-discrimination and equality, protect the vulnerable and advocate inclusiveness and participation in decision-making for all.

The major advantage of this approach is that it looks at development and communication in particular as a right and not a privilege. The import of looking at communication as a right is that it becomes an obligation on the part of the duty holders to perform their obligation and to the rights bearers to demand that right. When this is appreciated, it becomes very difficult for politicians to politicise these rights. Development initiatives are also rendered into sustainable projects that do not disappear with political regime change.

Understanding Karamoja and the Karimojong

The Karamoja region is understood today as a summation of three districts, namely: Kotido, Moroto and Nakapiripirit. It borders Kapchorwa and Kumi districts to the south; Katakwi and Lira districts to the southwest; Pader district to the west; and Kitgum district to the northwest. It also borders Sudan to the north and Kenya to the east and northeast.

Until the 1990s, Karamoja was one district and the second largest district in Uganda. At the size of approximately 27,200 sq. kms[5], Karamoja, has only a population of 920,498[6]. Thus Karamoja is a very big area with a very small population. While the geographical boundaries detach the Karimojong from their neighbours, history has indicated that the neighbours actually are "cousins" and share the same origin.

Historically, the Turkana, the Suk and the Iteso have the same background. They all moved together from Ethiopia (Abyassinia) to where they are now. When they arrived in present-day Karamoja, some people refused to leave and others left for several reasons, but their interest in cows played a major factor in their present location. Lack of pasture for their animals moved some down south and others eastwards in search of grass and water because the area has historically been dry.

However, others did not move. Those who stayed were called *Aikaramojang,* meaning failure to move because of age[7]. Those who moved to the southwest and settled in what is now the Teso area were presumably cursed by those who remained behind because they refused to stay with them. This group was called *Ates* (graves), implying that they had gone away from their elders and it would be difficult to trace their graves.

The intensification of drought in the area made life more difficult for those who had remained. The movement to the east into the present day Turkana area became inevitable. Interestingly this group went with the consent of those who remained. When good pasture and more land were eventually found in present day Kenya, they were praised for that and they were thus called *Aitur-Kwana,* with *Aitur* meaning *'praise'* and *Kwana* meaning *'now'.* It is now believed that the names of Turkana, Karimojong and the Ateso are corruptions of the Aitur-Kwana, Aika-amajong and Ateso respectively by the Europeans who could not pronounce the names properly.

The Socio-Economic, Political and Cultural Status of Karamoja and the Karimojong

Karamoja is characterised by insecurity, possession and misuse of illegal guns and general absence of law and order; unreliable water for production and human use; high illiteracy, poor health, and general economic backwardness.

There is also a dearth of socio-economic infrastructure; destructive attitudes and practices; environmental degradation; unreliable natural factors; weak political and administrative commitments; lack of recognition of the uniqueness of Karamoja; and prejudice against Karamoja by non-Karimojong. The sum total of these characteristics have contributed to the present confusion, problems and conflict in Karamoja.

Insecurity, Possession and Misuse of Illegal Guns

Insecurity in Karamoja is caused by two major factors, namely the position of illegal guns and the practice of cattle rustling and/or raiding. While the practice of cattle rustling is historical and can be argued to be part of "Karimojong culture", the recent acquisition of guns aggravated the situation by making the practice more lethal to both the Karimojong and their neighbours.

The practice of cattle rustling, which was limited to attacks in search of cattle, has now altered to include ransacking homesteads for food and property, murder, defilement and rape of the victims. This has led to destruction of the social and economic life of the victims and generally affected the neighbouring populations, resulting in their displacement into camps.

The districts that have mostly fallen prey to this Karimojong brutality are Katakwi and Kapchorwa where by early 2003 up to 88,000 people lived in internally displaced people's camps (IDPCs) for fear of attacks from marauding Karimojong rustlers. In these camps people face problems of shelter, medical care and sanitation, education for the children, malnutrition and starvation and general lack of adequate food.

The government policy of removing illegal guns from the Karimojong, popularly known as "disarmament", had started and gone on well for almost a year in 2002. Over 10,000 guns had been collected by the end of the year, out of the unknown but estimated 40,000 guns.

By the beginning of 2003, however, the whole process had hit a snag and rearmament went on as the government officials looked on. This was because the government itself, which had committed itself to disarmament, was unable to meet its part of the bargain, mainly the provision of security to the Karimojong against attacks from the Turkana and the Pokot from Kenya and from the other Karimojong who had not surrendered their guns.

Instead the government took away the UPDF that had been in Karamoja, and the Karimojong militias that had been recruited to protect the Karimojong, to fight elsewhere, particularly in northern Uganda to battle the rebels of the Lord's Resistance Army (LRA) led by Joseph Kony. All this increased the vulnerability of the Karimojong to their own and other external aggression. This vulnerability propelled and encouraged rearmament.

Absence of Law and Order in Karamoja

Part of the problem of Karamoja is that it has been administered, both by the colonial and post-colonial governments, as if it was not part of Uganda. The laws that apply to the rest of Uganda do not seem to apply to the Karimojong, and when they break them they are not punished according to the laws other Ugandans are familiar with.

State institutions like the police, the prisons and the courts either do not exist or where they exist, they are largely ineffective. The Karimojong largely administer their own "justice" that they consider appropriate to their culture and practice irrespective of whether or not it conforms to the rules of natural justice or are illegal. Revenge, vengeance and mob justice are the order of the day.

Unreliable Water for Animal and Human Use

Karamoja is a semi-arid region and it is the driest part of Uganda, with the lowest annual rainfall of 600 mm (25 inches) and the longest dry season of six months[9]. As in most dry areas of East Africa, pastoralism is the main activity as compared to arable agriculture.

The Karimojong practise transhumance during the dry season. When it rains, water becomes available but disappears quickly. Thus the area is in perpetual water shortage for crops, animals and human beings, except where there are water boreholes, and they are not that many in Karamoja.

The Conflict in Karamoja

The conflict in Karamoja revolves around cattle rustling in the form of raids and counter-raids within and ethnic communities within the region and with their neighbours. Cattle rustling, according the elders, started during the colonial period. The practice started as stock theft among the different pastoral clans within Karamoja and the pastoral communities in neighbouring Sudan and Kenya. These thieves moved at night in small numbers, and stole a few cattle using mainly spears and shield, bows and arrows. During these thefts, the thieves respected cultural norms. They did not kill children, women and the elderly indiscriminately.

In the late 1970s, the Karimojong acquired firearms, which changed the nature of the thefts. Cattle thefts evolved into cattle rustling as sophiscated guns replaced rudimental weapons. After the fall of Idi Amin's regime in 1979, the Karimojong in Matheniko, now Moroto district, entered the armoury in Moroto barracks and looted the weapons .

Those who could not have access to the armoury bought them from the fleeing soldiers. The unchecked inflow of guns and ammunition into Karamoja from the neighbouring areas including Sudan, Ethiopia and Kenya bolstered the capacity of the Karimojong to engage in massive raids.

Karimojong Raids and their Impact

There are several reasons given for cattle rustling that range from cultural, social to economic demands. Essentially cattle are the main source of wealth in Karamoja and a symbol of status in pastoral communities. The cow has generated a contradictory benefit to the Karamojong; on the one hand it is a source of livelihood and a basis for all economic, social and cultural rights such as the right to food, shelter, clothing, health and above all the right to have a family[9] but also has indirectly denied the Karimojong the right to development, access to health facilities, right to life, a clean and healthy environment, education and all civil and political rights because of insecurity and lack of the peace necessary for development.

Furthermore, the cows have ironically been the victims of the illegal gun because they also die during the raids, either in crossfire or from starvation and poor management, since veterinary services also are not extended to the communities *(manyattas)* because of the fear of the gun by veterinary personnel.

Consequently, Karamoja suffers the highest child death rates in the country. While Uganda's average infant mortality rate has fallen from 120 children per 1000 in 1988 to 81 children per 1000 in 2002, in Moroto district, for example, 147 children per 1000 do not live up to the age of one year and of the 800 surviving children out of 1000, 200 children do not reach the age of 5 years[10]. The doctors and other health workers out of fear of the gun in many *manyattas* are unable to take such health programmes as maternal care and immunisation to the villages of Karamoja.

It is not surprising that diseases such as scabies, which have long been eradicated in other parts of the country, still exist in Karamoja. Furthermore, while Karamoja has great tourist potential in Mount Kidepo National Park, for example, tourists do not visit the area because of the presence of illegal guns. Minerals such as gold, diamond and marble have not had serious investors to exploit them, again because of that fear.[11]

These are areas where information should be centred to protect what is left of Karimojong dignity. The Karimajong should be given opportunity and assisted to express their point of view and discuss among themselves and those who can engage them in charting the way forward for development.

The State of Communication in Karamoja

One of the indicators of poverty and backwardness is a poor communication network. The road network in Karamoja is all murram except in Moroto town. Until the beginning of 2003, there were only five telephone lines in the whole region of over 700,000 people and all of them were found in Moroto town.

In a report by one Remegio Achia, it was clearly stated that "While most Ugandans had managed to make their first telephone call, 99% of the Karamojong were still waiting to make one".[12] Unlike other regions, Karamoja is not served by electricity from Jinja. Private telephone coverage reached Karamoja after intense lobbying only in February 2003.[13]

According to the District Information officer, Moroto, Mr Mike Kidon-Onyang. There was an attempt by the government and NGOs to supply radios to Karamoja in 2000 during the disarmament programme. According to him, 300 radio sets were supplied in Kotido and some other 300 in Moroto and Nakapiripirit.

Later in 2001, the Ministry of Health (HIV/Aids Programme) distributed 80 radio sets in Moroto and another 80 in Kotido and Nakapiripirit. He further explained that there was only one radio, Radio Uganda , that is listened to in Karamoja from 4:00-5:00 daily for the Ng'akarimojong language. And that there was no FM radio station there yet, although Radio Veritas and Voice of Teso[14] were at times picked up in some parts of Karamoja.

Mr Kidon-Onyang explained how he, together with an Italian national, had been struggling to get a private FM radio set up in Karamoja since 1999, in vain:

> We went to Uganda Communications Commission to acquire frequency for Voice of Karamoja (FM Station). We failed because of two things: (i) we failed to raise the 5 million as rental fee to pay for the frequency; (ii) the man behind the wheel Dr Jovan , an Italian national,ended his work here, thereby leaving me helpless. Several other efforts were made to contact other possible funders. The European Union responded by giving some funds for the building of the radio house where I am staying waiting for assistance from nowhere... the house is ready but there is no equipment.[15]

The District Information Officer firmly believes that the presence of a radio in Moroto would make a tremendous contribution to not only ending the conflict there but to the development of Karamoja.

On 21st November 2003, the All Karamoja Radio FM (*Etoil NgiKarimajong*) 94.7 FM went on air. However, it is not clear how many of the Karimojong have benefited from this facility. It can be through the adoption of a human rights-based approach to communication in a place like Karamoja that the needs, demands and concerns of people like Kidon-Onyang can be addressed and monitored.

A Human Rights Approach-Based Communication

As indicated above, human rights-based communication is predicated on several broad principles, namely: explicit recognition of the international human rights normative framework; accountability, non-discrimination and equality; participation, empowerment and special attention to the most vulnerable groups.

Express Recognition of the Right to Communicate as a Human Right

The right to communicate as a human right is not yet enshrined in international human rights law but there are ongoing efforts in that direction, and a debate is raging on, as to whether a declaration should not be adopted on the "Right to Communicate."[16] The pressure to have a "right to communicate" is born out of the realisation that the media, under neo-liberal policies and owing to the inability of the state to respond to the demands of the population, rather than to the demands of finance capital, are becoming increasingly homogenised to the point where the minority, dissenting or even local voices and issues are not being heard. Making communication a right imposes on the state the obligation to respect, promote and fulfil its duty to the rights holders.

Nonetheless, in the absence of such a specific right to communicate, there is still an existing rights framework where the right can be situated and where it is inherently grounded. The right to communicate would include the totality of freedom of opinion, expression and more importantly, the right to receive information from both state and private sources.

Key elements of this right include the right to diverse, pluralistic media; equitable access to the means of communication, as well as the media; the right to practise and express one's culture, including the right to use the language of one's choice; the right to participate in the public decision-making process; the right to access information, including from public bodies; the right to be free from undue restrictions on the content of information; and privacy rights, including the right to communicate anonymously; the unfettered right to hold opinions and the right to express and disseminate any information or ideas.

The right to communicate is located in several international instruments. Article 19 of the Universal Declaration of Human Rights sates:

> Everyone has a right to freedom of opinion and expression; this right includes the right to hold opinions without interference and to seek, receive and impart information and ideas through any media and regardless of frontiers.[17]

Furthermore Article 19 of the International Covenant on Civil and Political Rights provides for the freedom of opinion, expression and information. It states:

> Everyone shall have the right to hold opinions without interference... Everyone shall have the right to freedom of expression; this right shall include the freedom to seek, receive and impart information and ideas of all kinds, regardless of frontiers, either orally, in writing or in print, in the form of art or through any other media of his choice. ..The exercise of the rights provided for... carries with it special duties and responsibilities. It may therefore be subject to certain restrictions, but these shall only be such as are provided by law and are necessary:
>
> (a) For respect of the rights or reputations of others;
>
> (b) For the protection of national security or of public order (order public) or of public health or morals.

This right is further enshrined in Article 13(1) of the African Charter on Human and People's Rights (ACHR) and in article 10(1) of the European Commission of Human Rights (ECHR). The Constitution of the Republic of Uganda also recognises the right to information[18].

This means therefore that the Karimojong must be empowered to demand to communicate as a right rather than as a privilege. As of now Karimojong society remains hierarchical and respectful of elders and leaders to level of not questioning or raising an opinion contrary to that of the leader or elder.

Until this stereotype is broken, information and communication will remain one-way (by the sender) without substantive feedback from the recipients so that the latter can avoid being branded rebellious. It is not even agreed that the information by the leaders is always quality information. It is known that during the disarmament programmes, some leaders were being accused of abetting cattle rustling and discouraging their subjects from handing in the guns.

The Obligation of the State to Guarantee the Right to Communication

In general terms, Article 19 prohibits the state from interfering in these rights by taking such steps as are necessary to make freedom of expression a reality for every one. This includes taking legislative or other regulatory steps as well as practical positive measures, for example through the establishment of public communication centres.

More practically, states that are party to the Universal Declaration of Human Rights as a matter of international customary law, and to the International Covenant on Civil and Political Rights (ICCPR), which Uganda ratified in 1995, are bound by it. Practical measures that can be taken include creating conditions to ensure media autonomy and pluralism.

What is Expected of Uganda-as a State Party to ICCPR and ACHR?

Under international human rights law, the State is expected to address the "right to communicate" on three major levels, namely *to respect, protect* and *fulfil them*. All these can be achieved through legislative and administrative /policy measures put in place by the government.

Media pluralism entails ensuring that all groups in a given society (including Karamoja) have access to the media. The conditions in a given area should be such that communication media are open to all without discrimination and that there are no individuals or groups that are excluded from access to such media. It also means enjoyment of freedom of expression, which includes freedom to use such a media.

The obligation to *respect* means that Uganda, for example, should not take any measures that result in preventing people's access to information or inhibit communication. The obligation to *protect* means that the state must take positive measures to ensure that enterprises or individuals do not deprive citizens of their access to information or stifle their right to communicate.

This entails various measures to enhance media pluralism, including positive measures to increase the media outlets and diversify and improve the content of information for communication. It requires therefore that the state party to the Covenant on Civil and Political Rights, for example, take practical positive measures to create an environment in which the media, and diverse information content, can flourish.

Specific measures required will differ depending on circumstances on the ground in an area. In general terms, however, the measures would include setting up non-discriminatory media subsidy schemes, adopting rules on local content, encouraging community broadcasting, providing tax breaks for new media outlets and promoting local content production.

There are also indirect measures that would be taken which would have a positive impact on the media pluralism such as ensuring constant supply of the goods necessary for different media, such as electricity or newsprint, promoting modern communication technologies and providing modern communications technologies and adequate training opportunities.[19]

The obligation to fulfil incorporates both an obligation to *facilitate* and an obligation to *provide*. In other words whenever, for example, an individual or group is unable, for reasons beyond their control, to enjoy the right to communicate, including the right to information and expression through the means at their disposal or because of conditions beyond their control (e.g. those who are too poor to afford radios, TV sets or are illiterate, dumb etc), states have the duty to provide the information, radios, TVs, telephones using all the means available, free of charge. States can solicit international assistance, if feasible.

Ensuring Accountability in Rights-Based Communication

Once it is clear that the right to communication is grounded in rights/ entitlements, not privileges, and therefore carries obligations and that the rights holder can claim the entitlement, then issues of accountability follow. This requires that adequate laws, policies and mechanisms of readiness and accountability that can deliver on entitlements are in place.

These should respond to denial and violations and ensure accountability. Furthermore, universal standards must be translated into locally determinant benchmarks for measuring progress and enhancing accountability. While everything is not achieved in one day, there must be a clear plan, showing targets in a specific time. It is these benchmarks that will help in the monitoring process. For example how many Karimojong will have had radios by 2010?

Duty bearers must have both the political will and the means to ensure delivery of entitlements. They must put in place the necessary legislative, administrative and institutional mechanisms required to achieve that aim. The international community must be called in for effective international co-operation, especially where there are shortages of resources and capacities in developing institutions/countries.

Right to Communication for the Karimojong

Whatever programme has to be made for Karamoja, it must be of the Karimojong and by the Karimojong. That way it becomes sustainable. The programmes must focus on beneficiaries as owners of rights and directors of development.

Emphasis must be laid on human beings as the centre of the development process – through their advocates and NGOs. The objective is to give power and capacity so that the Karimojong are able to change their own lives, improve their own communities and influence their own future.

Participation is an important civil and political right. It is necessary that the planning process engenders and encourages a high degree of participation including from communities, civil society, ministries, indigenous people, women and others. Participation must be active and meaningful. Mere ceremonial contacts with beneficiaries are not sufficient. It is not enough to provide information. Information must be of high quality and discussion and feedback should show that participation was meaningful.

In the planning process for Karamoja, for example, particular attention should be given to non-discrimination, equality, equity and vulnerable groups among the Karimojong. Some of the problems and conflicts in Karamoja arise out of government neglect and marginalisation of the region. Not all Karimojong, however, are vulnerable and have been neglected.

The conventional vulnerable groups include but are not limited to children, women, minorities, indigenous peoples and prisoners. It is important to realise that there is no universal checklist of who is most vulnerable at any given time, in every context.

Rights-based approaches require that such questions be answered locally: Who is vulnerable here and now? Who should be heard here and now? Who needs what information here? This helps to ensure that people in need are helped as a right, not as charity.

Conclusion

The article has suggested that the Karamoja region lacks information and is generally underdeveloped. It is the least developed region in the country by all indicators. The possession of illegal guns has exacerbated the problem.

Several regimes, from colonialism to date, have failed to resolve the problem. It is suggested that part of the problem has been failure of the state to appreciate that transforming Karamoja requires an appreciation of development as a right and that developing Karamoja is an obligation of the State.

It is also critical for the Karimojong to know that development is a right and an entitlement that they need to claim. However, claiming this right can only become reality if people enjoy the right to communication, which includes the right to information. To fully enjoy this right, the principles of a rights-based approach, namely accountability, empowerment, participation, attention to the vulnerable and non-discrimination, have to be respected. This way the planning, programming, budgeting and policies for Karamoja, in peace and in conflict, will have better results exist than currently.

Notes

[1]   Bataringaya Security Report on Karamoja, 1961-Quoted in "A Proposal to Establish Karamoja Disarmament and Development Secretariat (KDDS)", 1st May 2003. All the successive governments, from the colonial one up to the present government, have not succeeded in defeating these "thieves' even when the various successive governments have had superior power over the Karimojong.

[2]   See infra.

[3]   "Duty bearers"are those with obligations or responsibilities for the realisation of rights. In the traditional legal sense the state is always taken to be the sole duty bearer. My view however is that it is a responsibility of all parties, partners to contribute to the realisation of rights as a moral duty and social responsibility.

4   "Rights holders" at a conceptual level include are everybody with a right depending on the issue at hand.

5   See Report of the Office of the Prime Minister (OPM); Karamoja Disarmament Programme (2005-2006).

6 See *"Karamoja: Searching for Peace and Human Rights"*- A Report of the Uganda Human Rights Commission, 2004 p.6-7 (Statistics from UBOS 2002).

7 See A. Nsibambi & F. Byarugaba "Problems of Political and Administrative Participation in a Semi-Arid area of Uganda: A Case Study of Karamoja" in *The African Review, A Journal of African Politics Development and International Affairs* Vo. 9 Number 2, 1982 p80.

8 Ibid p.79.

9 The Karimojong have to pay hundreds of head of cattle as bride price.

10 See President Yoweri Museveni's Circular to All Political Leaders and Military Commanders in the Karamoja Region on Guidelines on Mobilisation for the Disarmament Exercise in Karamoja Region dated 9th December 2001

11 Ibid.

12 Remegio Achia, "Overview of the Karamoja Strategic Workshop" that took place on 17th –19 May 2002 at Leslona and Mount Moroto Hotels p.6.

13 I was in Karamoja when MTN network was launched (2004) and there was excessive excitement among the elite there.

14 Even these programmes started barely two years ago (2000).

15 An interview in my office on 26th June 2003 at the UHRC.

16 See Statement on the Right to Communicate by Article 19 Global Campaign for Free Expression, London February 2003.

17 Universal Declaration of Human Rights, 1948.

18 Article 41 of the Constitution of the Republic of Uganda (1995).

19 See Statement on the Right to Communicate by Article 19 Global Campaign for Free Expression, London Feb.2003 p.2.

6

Media, Peace-building, and the Culture of Violence

George W. Lugalambi

There is wide agreement today that far from being a crisis confined to the violence and mayhem instigated by the so-called Lord's Resistance Army (LRA), the conflict in northern Uganda has everything to do with the political economy of the region in general.[1] The public and the media have been baffled by the persistence of this conflict, its destructiveness, and its apparent immunity from resolution. The government's early insistence on a military rather than political solution seems to have been misguided as it poisoned the atmosphere for the subsequent attempts at a peaceful settlement. However wishy-washy the attempts at a negotiated settlement have been, the fact that this conflict has become so intractable is not an aberration. In this chapter, I will argue that the LRA conflict and indeed all types of conflict need to be understood fundamentally in three contexts: the first concerns the nature of conflict in society; the second concerns the political culture of violence; and the third is about violence as built into the structure of the political economy.

The Ugandan government has been facing off with insurgents of the LRA since 1988 in a conflict that now appears to meet the conditions of intractability. The LRA, a Christian fundamentalist group whose professed mission is to establish a government based on the biblical Ten Commandments, has visited ghastly violence upon the population of northern Uganda. Its crimes against humanity include abducting children and adults and forcing them into fighting, as well as killing, raping, maiming, and displacing countless numbers of people. The LRA is also listed on the US government's Terrorism Exclusion List.[2]

As Coleman (2000) points out, intractable conflicts persist for long without resolution, tending to escalate, transform, and flare up intermittently. They culminate in an interminably high degree of intensity and devastation. Typically, intractable conflicts simmer in a complex web of issues rooted in historical, religious, cultural, political, and economic factors. Those who have experienced and observed the LRA will agree that intractable conflicts "give rise to a threat to basic human needs or values and result in destructive outcomes ranging from mutual alienation and contempt to mutual atrocities" (Coleman, 2000, p. 428) between those waging the conflict and those trapped in its path.

Nature of Conflict

In a functional society, the constructive management of conflict lies at the heart of the task of governance. If this premise is accepted, then the idea that conflict is an indispensable element of society, a central feature of social existence and progress (Nathan, 2000; Brand-Jacobsen, 2000; Nnoli, 1998) is not as heretical as it might sound. As far as Africa is concerned, what appears to confound many people is the nature of the conflicts raging on the continent. According to Tandon (2000), "even if there are 'good' reasons for conflicts, there are no 'good' reasons why these conflicts degenerate into violence and brutality that shame humanity" (p. 166). Nnoli (1998) understands conflict as the contradictions born of dissimilarities in "interests, ideas, ideologies, orientations, perceptions and tendencies" (p. 6). Since human affairs are basically about these kinds of differences, Nnoli (1998) concurs too that the real problem with conflict is its eruption into violence.

This perspective on conflict has implications for the way the media think about the causes of violence and how they engage with the process of peacebuilding. Therefore, the tendency to conceive of conflict solely in terms of violence leads to the erroneous assumption that where there is no direct and visible violence, there necessarily is no conflict (Brand-Jacobsen, 2000). As a result, the media, policy-makers, politicians, the international community, and the public are often easily drawn to the violent outcomes of a conflict. However, the eruption of violence typically signifies that a conflict has been poorly managed, for example, by ignoring it and by intervening half-heartedly or through misguided strategies. It is for this reason that following Galtung (1969), scholars have maintained the distinctions among different forms of violence: "direct," "structural," and "cultural" (Brand-Jacobsen, 2000; Opotow, 2000).

Differences in Violence

Direct or personal violence is tangible in that it appears in the form of physical acts like war, assault, sexual abuse, killing, and armed confrontation. Conversely, structural violence is latent in that it is embedded within the social, political, and economic systems of a society, community, country, and the world. Structural violence is embodied in the disparities in "the allocation of goods, resources, and opportunities, between different groups, classes, genders, nationalities, etc., because of the structure governing their relationship" (Brand-Jacobsen, 2000 p. 17).

The obscure nature of structural violence makes it difficult to decipher and to link to its direct manifestations, yet it contributes substantially to the intractability of conflicts. According to Galtung (1969), structural violence "shows up as unequal power and consequently as unequal life chances" (p. 171) owing to the skewed distribution of resources like education, health, and income. Apartheid, patriarchy, slavery, colonialism, imperialism, and globalisation have been cited as emblematic of structural violence. This type of violence is no less insidious or harmful than direct violence. In fact it is often more catastrophic if one considers the lives lost and human suffering resulting from investment in the production of armaments as opposed to goods and services that would save and improve lives (Brand-Jacobsen, 2000; Galtung, 1969).

Cultural violence refers to those elements of a culture that legitimise the use of violence as a way of dealing with conflict. Let us stay with Uganda's political culture as an example. From colonial times through the postcolonial era, violence and coercion have been institutionalised as mechanisms to deal with conflict, thus undercutting the development and deepening of democratic values and supporting political norms (Mittelman, 1975; Makara & Tukahebwa, 1996; Ocitti, 2000). Much of the political violence in Uganda is attributable to the systematic denial of the people's right to organise in pursuit of their collective interests. This partly has to do with the larger failure and difficulty to manage the competition for power. Yet the right to organise, in whichever form including as political parties, and for whatever purpose including opposing state policies or actions, is indispensable for citizens to be able to hold their government, politicians, and policy-makers democratically accountable (Mamdani, 1995).

Judging from the contested discourse about the role of political parties in Uganda, the tendency of those in power to conflate political opposition and legitimate dissent with subversion reflects a narrow, self-serving, and unsophisticated understanding of conflict. While there is strong ground to indict Uganda's traditional political parties for their harmful contribution to the systemic crises the country has experienced, the evaluation of their performance, as Mamdani (1995) contends, has to be balanced with consideration of the underlying principles of pluralistic politics.

Managing Conflict

In a comparative assessment of the emergence of competitive party politics in Uganda and in the West, Apter (1961) concluded that for political parties in Western democracies, free and open conflict "is a source of strength in democracy" (p. 301). In this context, the function of conflict is to pinpoint grievances that need to be addressed. Looking at Uganda's experience from a perspective of basic democratic principles, the problem with political parties is not that they are inherently unworkable as those currently in control of state power claim; nor is it that they are necessarily a panacea for the historical crisis of democracy as their proponents claim. Rather, the problem with political parties is symptomatic of a deeper failure of governance reflected in systemically dysfunctional approaches to conflict management. This failure of governance typifies a political culture in which violence and coercion have emerged as the norm.

Thus, what arguably is at issue is not so much the prevalence of conflict as the question of how to deal with it justly, democratically, and productively. Violent conflict, Nnoli (1998) tells us, grows out of the failure to accommodate and resolve differences using institutional arrangements and procedures that could eradicate or mitigate the negative consequences of these contradictions while making the most of their positive corollaries. Hence, "conflict resolution boils down to the creation of the conditions that will enable conflicting forces to accept these arrangements and procedures" (Nnoli, 1998, p. 6).

In states where the human, institutional, and material resources to settle disputes and grievances, to moderate competition, and to safeguard people's rights and security are scarce or absent, individuals and groups may opt for direct violence (Nathan, 2000) to assert their claims. Successive Ugandan governments too have had the predilection to resort to direct violence to assert their authority and to exclude other individual and organised interests from the political process. When direct violence is used in response to contested issues or conflicts that are essentially political, then the scenario we are talking about is that of political violence, which Mittelman (1975) defines as "the utilisation of force to maintain or upset the prevailing mode of allocating values authoritatively" (p. 195).

Peace and Peacebuilding

Brand-Jacobsen (2000) contends that the way we understand violence is instrumental to the way we think about peace and peacebuilding. In this sense, the expectations we have of society in general are the same expectations we have of the media. For example, as a response to direct violence, the media can help society to identify and promote direct acts aimed at propping up peace and transforming conflicts. These include dialogue and conscientious pursuit of non-violence by exposing and opposing injustices, oppression, violent behaviour, and aggression at all levels of society and in all social domains (home, school, workplace, and so on).

In response to structural violence, the media can help society to identify the structures of peace necessary to cater for the people's needs and opportunities for them to individually and collectively realise their full potential. This also includes those structures needed to ensure respect and protection of the rights of everybody or every group. In response to cultural violence, the media can help society to identify the cultures of peace whereby peace is cherished as a value. This goes along with honouring and celebrating differences as well as safeguarding the political, civil, social, economic, and cultural rights of all individuals, groups, and communities in society. Even if these responses to violence were based on the principles of conflict prevention (Ackermann, 2003, pp. 341-342), the logic of "structural prevention" of violence would require long-term strategies that integrate measures designed to establish democratic governance, ensure respect for human rights, allow civil society to grow, and foster economic, social, and political stability. This would be different from "operational prevention", whose aim would be to tackle pending and unfolding crises as in the case of humanitarian intervention.

Collier and Hoeffler (2002) demonstrate in their economic model of civil war that violent conflict in sub-Saharan Africa is a contingent effect of poor economic performance. However, one should not go away with the impression that direct violence is excusable in situations where the structural causes of violence such as economic deprivation admittedly remain intact to a large extent. For as Tandon (2000) argues, "growth or no growth, a culture of non-violence and respect for ethnic pluralism need to be cultivated and nourished in their own right" (p.167).

Thus far, the central points of this analysis have been that: (a) there is no essential linkage between conflict and violence. When conflict is properly managed, which is a function of governance, it can strengthen the democratic process by bringing contested issues out into the open so they can be projected onto the public agenda and addressed; (b) violence, and political violence in particular, has persisted in Uganda precisely because there is a culture that endorses or tolerates the use of violence to settle political questions and other differences; and (c) on top of interventions aimed at eroding the culture of violence, sustainable peacebuilding necessitates strategies aimed at progressively dismantling the structural elements of violence.

Media in Perspective

Having established a conceptual orientation that separates out forms of violence in terms of their specific characteristics and identifies the relationships among these forms, we can now locate the media within this conceptual matrix. From this point on, I will assign the media a cultural role in peacebuilding and in the management of conflict as well as in the prevention of violence. The attempt to focus media attention on the culture of violence comes from the observation that the conventions of the media draw journalists almost by instinct towards direct violence at the expense of peacebuilding and the cultural factors that make it possible for violent conflict to thrive.

The contribution of the media to promoting peace is a subject of debate. This is understandable given that journalists are not autonomous agents holding up a mirror for society to see reality or the truth. Rather, as Carruthers (2000) observes, news and the entire package of media output are shaped by journalists' values as well as the ideological dispositions and institutional norms of the structures through which their work is organised. Becker (1982) has suggested that peace, to begin with, does not appeal to the media, a situation that was also reflected in the absence of empirical data about the media portrayal of peace. Jacobson and Jang (2002) have also proposed that the media may actually encourage war and violence because of the profit motive that drives newsgathering towards sensational stories that focus on superfluous and wanton violence. In the process, the news about violent conflict gets treated so simplistically that it leaves the public misinformed.

In some instances, the media have adopted what I consider to be counter-productive and illusionary neutral stances. Irrespective of the length to which journalists might go in trying to project their presumed neutrality, violent conflict by definition provokes and disturbs the values that undergird the sense we make of ourselves as a society. For that matter, when the media contrive to remain neutral in the face of violent conflict, they effectively undermine the moral imperative of their work. When neutrality is rationalised especially on the grounds that journalists must strike a balance in their reporting of a conflict, they may unwittingly create the impression of a "moral equivalence" (Carruthers, 2000, p. 241) between the parties involved.

Understanding Media

Just as the impact of the media on public policy in general remains a moot question, so is their effect on peacebuilding. The disputed notion of the "CNN effect" is often used to test the media-policy relationship particularly in foreign affairs (Livingstone, 2000). This notion is relevant to intra-state peace processes as well because foreign policy in many instances revolves around issues of peacebuilding and conflict such as negotiation of peace settlements, intervention in humanitarian crises, and containment of violence within states. In Robinson's (2000) "policy-media interaction model", the CNN effect is about the conditions under which media coverage may succeed or fail to influence the foreign policies of major Western powers. I am, however, adapting and extending elements of this idea to apply beyond the realm of Western foreign policy towards conflict management.

As an example, the media in a country like Uganda may so "frame" their coverage of a conflict as to empathise with those who bear the brunt of violence and its effects by portraying them as victims. In this kind of framing, the government may be implicitly or explicitly criticized for not aggressively initiating and following through with a peaceful resolution to a conflict. On the other hand, journalists may report on a conflict by keeping emotionally aloof from it. The framing effect of this kind of detachment may be to implicitly endorse the position of one side or the other; and usually the dominant party, which tends to be the government, has the greater muscle to shape its position and to ensure that this position is represented. These media practices have implications for peacebuilding in Uganda because governments and their adversaries in violent conflict are more often than not inclined to respond militarily and violently rather than peacefully and democratically.

While the concept of the CNN effect assumes that the media force governments to act against their will or in ways they ordinarily would not, I employ the idea broadly to underline the perceived power of the media to influence the decisions of different political actors in a conflict. However, although it is intuitive to think of the media as having a powerful influence on the decisions that determine the course of a conflict, Jakobsen (2000) argues that thinking about media influence in terms of direct cause-and-effect blurs the indirect and indiscernible but bigger effect of the media coverage of conflict. The real impact of the media is disguised in their editorial and news production values. For example, the media often ignore conflicts before they break out into violence and after the hostilities have ended. Moreover, even when they are covering the violent phase of a conflict, the media tend to be decidedly selective. One of the consequences of these media approaches to covering conflict is to turn the attention away from long-term measures aimed at preventing conflicts from becoming violent to short-term interventions (Jakobsen, 2000). This reinforces the public and media's own tendency to focus on direct violence at the expense of the cultural and structural dimensions of violence.

Sensitivity to Media

Clearly, the history of violent conflict in Uganda suggests that governments are invariably sensitive to the influence that the media have on public perceptions of their effectiveness or competence in resolving conflicts and on public attributions of responsibility for their causes and solutions. This is why the current Ugandan government, like those that preceded it, demands and expects the compliance of the media, especially when it is under pressure. This has usually been the case whenever things have tended to boil over during confrontations with armed groups. In Africa, media freedom is at its most precarious when governments are politically distressed (Lugalambi, 2003), which happens particularly when governments are faced with armed political challenges. This has implications for the quality of information that the public gets during situations of violent conflict. Yet, if ever there was a need for robust, independent journalism, situations of armed conflict present the strongest case for such journalism. The reason is that in underdeveloped democracies, there is not the kind of civilian control and public scrutiny of the military as there is in the advanced democracies. In the absence of democratic scrutiny, the military has often been injudicious in handling conflicts.

Ugandans by and large concur that the LRA's behaviour is out of sync with the grievances it is claiming. But the military too has sometimes been censured for its high-handed and indiscriminate response to the conflict. In the aftermath of the September 11, 2001, attacks in the US, the designation of the LRA as a terrorist group provided the government with new justifications in its fight against the rebels and those it imagines as being sympathetic to their cause. Freedom House said in its *Annual Survey of Press Freedom 2002* that terrorism had given some governments a rationale to deal harshly with the media.[3]

The Ugandan government has routinely suppressed the media. However, judging by its own rhetoric about its record on free speech, many people probably did not expect the government to stop the publication of a newspaper altogether at this point in the democratisation process. On October 10, 2002, the country's main independent daily, *The Monitor*, published a story claiming that an army combat helicopter had crashed under unclear circumstances while fighting the LRA. Beyond the specifics of the story, the wider and touchy implication was that the chopper had been shot down during operations that the government was keen to portray to the public as its toughest and ultimate offensive against this protracted insurgency.

The military vehemently denied the story. The ensuing police raid of the newsrooms, offices, and production facilities of *The Monitor* in search of the source of the story shut it down for a week. This prompted speculation and concerns that the government intended to ban the paper. A military spokesman, Lt Paddy Ankunda, referred to the story as "a kind of psychological terrorism" for which the newspaper would have to answer.[4] The foreign affairs minister, James Wapakhabulo, responded to the US government concerns about the fate of independent media in Uganda following action against *The Monitor* by echoing the US's own national security advisor Condoleezza Rice. In October 2001, Rice exhorted the US media not to broadcast or publish Osama bin Laden's speeches without screening them for inflammatory material or coded messages. As Wapakhabulo put it:

> Uganda shares the position of the US that the fight against terrorism requires firm and deliberate action and it was on the basis of this belief that the US government advised media houses to desist from publishing and reproducing propaganda emanating from the Qatar-based Al Jazeera television station which was being used by Al Qaeda terrorists.[5]

In mid 2003, when the LRA extended their attacks to eastern Uganda, the government closed a local station, Radio Kyoga Veritas FM, "accusing it of broadcasting alarmist news about the attacks of the Lord's Resistance Army rebels in Teso sub-region."[6]

The merits and demerits of these media reports and the reactions they touched off in the government, the military, and the public need not concern us too much at this moment. The relevance of these two examples is in the light they shed on the observation by Bruck and Roach (1993) that the media provide the information environment in which we derive our perceptions of the world around us. Therefore, the nature of coverage that media audiences encounter has a critical impact on people's political effectiveness and their perception of how important peace issues are to the political agenda and the life of a society in general.

Media Marginalises Peace

The problem though, as suggested earlier, remains that matters of peace are barely covered in the media. The reasons have been traced back to the very organisation and structure of the media system and its influence on the production of media content. Even when journalists individually and by their own initiative or enterprise are willing to challenge the conventions of their trade, they find that they have to pit their conscience against the corporate culture in which they work. As Tehranian (2002) contends, "most journalists tend to be moral agents caught in immoral predicaments" (p. 75). Besides, the news production codes of the media privilege the dramatic and the sensational over issues that evolve gradually or through a process.

Since peace is a process rather than a fixed condition (Bruck and Roach, 1993), the media cannot meaningfully capture the process of peacebuilding episodically, that is, by spotlighting developments as bounded events or series of occurrences with a definite beginning and end. The view that the majority of Ugandans get their news from radio has been held for a long time. But while our understanding of the impact of radio on political cognition remained largely intuitive, evidence has emerged in recent years suggesting that the principal media in Africa – radio, television, and newspapers, in that order – interact variously with interpersonal contacts to influence public opinion (Afrobarometer, 2003). Because of this assumed interaction among different media forms, on the one hand, and between mass media and interpersonal contacts, on the other, what we know about a particular medium can give us useful clues regarding public opinion on collective political preferences.

For example, we can extrapolate from Iyengar's (1991) study of television news in the US in which he examined the effect of "episodic" and "thematic" news formats, known as "frames", on how viewers attribute responsibility for political issues and how these news frames indirectly affect public opinion. To frame news episodically is to concentrate on particular events or cases, whereas to frame news thematically is to present issues and events within a broad context. The problem with the tendency towards episodic framing is that issues like peacebuilding that do not lend themselves to packaging as specific happenings are hardly a priority for coverage; and that is if, for starters, they get considered at all. The media's emphasis on episodic framing of news particularly affects the way news is selected for television and how the public assigns responsibility for given political issues. According to Iyengar (1991, pp. 2-3):

> Exposure to episodic news makes viewers less likely to hold public officials accountable for the existence of some problem and also less likely to hold them responsible for alleviating it. By discouraging viewers from attributing responsibility for national issues to political actors, television decreases the public's control over their elected representatives and the policies they pursue.

The attribution of responsibility is considered essential for citizens to exercise civic control over those in power, and the way issues are framed in television news significantly impacts such attributions (Iyengar, 1991). There are compelling reasons to infer that these patterns observed in the packaging of television news apply to a substantial degree to the media in general. This is because there are common patterns behind news production values across all media forms and systems, and many studies have examined and confirmed these patterns (Gans, 1979; Gitlin, 1980).

Traditional Journalism

Media scholars have found that the media's traditional approaches to news are particularly at odds with the process of peacebuilding. Wolfsfeld (1997) studied the role of the Israeli news media in the Middle East conflict and concluded that the relationship between the goals of the peace process and the journalists' professional routines were so contradictory that the media were in fact formidable impediments to peace efforts in Israel. He describes a news environment characterised by a virtually irreconcilable polarisation separating the values of peace from the values of the media.

For instance, Wolfsfeld (1997) contends that whereas peacebuilding is complex, journalists want events and issues that are straightforward; whereas peacebuilding may evolve gradually and uneventfully, journalists yearn for activity and instant outcomes; whereas negotiations for peace generally proceed in a dreary process, journalists are obsessed with drama. Furthermore, while success in peacebuilding results in a thaw of tensions, conflict remains the staple of journalism; and while it is inevitable that the critical aspects of a peace process will happen out of the public and media's sight, for journalists what matters are information and access.

Nonetheless, Wolfsfeld (1997) still believes that despite their negative impact, the media are just as capable of making a positive contribution to the peace process. In any case, the media can either glorify or puncture the images of the parties to a conflict, infuse optimistic or pessimistic impressions about the possibilities of peace, fortify or undermine the public's willingness to compromise, and buttress or render hollow the legitimacy of the protagonists in a conflict including the state.

Media's Social Mandate

While questions linger over the issue of whether the media can promote peace, we can only begin to settle these questions by linking peacebuilding to the media's social mandate; or the idea of journalism implemented with a social purpose. In a previous exploration of how the media can help prevent conflict, I floated five generic roles for the media (Lugalambi,

2001). I consider these roles to be as germane to peacebuilding as they are to conflict prevention, and I will briefly interpret and summarise them here.

The first role, that is, nurturing the public interest, compels the media to champion a common vision based on those core principles and values around which citizens ought to be encouraged to unite. The second role, namely, cultivating public consensus, is about the media helping to focus citizens' attention on issues of collective concern, to generate agreement, and to persuade people to voice their opinions. The third role, that is, feeling the pulse of public opinion, requires that the media constantly provide a kind of social intelligence that captures the essence of citizens' perceptions of issues at stake, thus identifying points of tension before they crack. The fourth role, namely, directing the current of public opinion, makes it incumbent upon the media to articulate the concerns of those who may disagree with the dominant thinking but whose claims are nevertheless as legitimate as those held by the majority. And the fifth role, which is that of critical engagement with issues, compels the media to rigorously inquire into the motives of all the parties to a conflict with an eye to establishing and challenging those tendencies that might ruin peacebuilding efforts.

Underlying the journalistic strategies implicit in the five roles specified above is the idea that the media can support peacebuilding by proactively working against those elements of the political culture that enable the institutionalisation of violence. This approach to reporting puts greater weight on the social mechanisms and democratic values that are needed to entrench the culture of peace as an essential part of the political culture. Meaningful democracy presupposes the existence of a political culture in which peacebuilding is a central feature of the process of democratisation.

Conflict activists, practitioners, and analysts have developed and proposed an array of important functions or roles that the media in Africa may take on in helping to prevent, resolve, and manage conflicts (Onadipe and Lord, 1998; Manoff, 1998; Hieber, 1998). The essence of my argument, however, is that the media can best promote peacebuilding by focusing their attention on those aspects of the political culture that create the environment for violence in the first place. I submit that it is the culture of violence that creates the conditions for the undemocratic and violently authoritarian responses to political conflict both by those in power and those opposed to them.

Peace is not a tangible condition that should be reduced to or equated with the absence of direct violence. Rather, it is a way of life and a social attitude that affects collective democratic behaviour. We should be able to talk about evolving a culture of peace the way we talk about dismantling the culture of violence. Uganda as a society must find ways of nurturing a culture of peace by creating democratic institutions and systems of governance for arbitrating conflicts. With these structures and their accompanying norms in place, people will have less reason to resort to violence when dealing with political conflicts. The media can contribute to the development of norms of peace within Uganda's political culture.

Conclusion

This chapter has elaborated the characteristics of conflict and violence, making the point that although conflicts are endemic to human interaction, they do not have to be violent. For that matter, Uganda as a society has to work hard through its social institutions like the media at fostering the culture of peace within the broader political culture. Various reasons have been advanced to explain why it is easier and more practical for the media to focus on violent conflict than to communicate about peace and peacebuilding. These problems notwithstanding, the Ugandan media are duty-bound to promote a political culture that shuns violence in favour of peaceful and democratic solutions to legitimate differences.

Notes

1 See for example the related issues raised in a seminar by Conciliation Resources (London), the Centre of African Studies (University of London), and Kacoke Madit (London) at
http://www.c-r.org/pubs/occ_papers/Learning_Uganda.shtml Retrieved July 17, 2003.
2 See US Department of State Fact Sheet at http://www.state.gov/s/ct/rls/fs/ 2002/15222.htm Retrieved July 17, 2003.
3 See the Freedom House 2002 report in the section titled, "The Press: Marksman and Target in the War on Terrorism" at http://www.freedomhouse.org/ pfs2002/pfs2002.pdf Retrieved August 18, 2003.
4 See "Army Denies Losing Chopper", *The New Vision*, October 11, 2002.
5 See "Wapa[khabulo] Defends Action on Monitor", *The New Vision*, October 14, 2002.
6 See "Museveni Closed Soroti FM Radio", *The Monitor*, July 20, 2003.

References

Ackermann, A. 2003. "The Idea and Practice of Conflict Prevention." *Journal of Peace Research* 40: 339-347.

Afrobarometer, 2003. "Freedom of Speech, Media Exposure, and the Defense of a Free Press in Africa." Afrobarometer Briefing Paper No. 7. http://www.afrobarometer.org/papers/AfrobriefNo7.pdf Retrieved August 18, 2003.

Apter, D. E. 1961. *The Political Kingdom in Uganda: A Study of Bureaucratic Nationalism.* London, UK: Frank Cass.

Becker, J. 1982. "Communication and Peace: The Empirical and Theoretical Relations Between Two Categories in Social Science." *Journal of Peace Research* 19: 227-240.

Brand-Jacobsen, K. F. 2000. "Peace: The Goal and the Way." In *Searching for Peace: The Road to Transcend*, eds. J. Galtung, C. G. Jacobsen and K. F. Brand-Jacobsen, 16-24. London, UK: Pluto Press.

Bruck, P., and Roach, C. 1993. "Dealing with Reality: The News Media and the Promotion of Peace." In *Communication and Culture in War and Peace*, ed. C. Roach, 71-96. Newbury Park, CA: Sage Publications.

Carruthers, S. L. 2000. *The Media at War: Communication and Conflict in the Twentieth Century.* New York, NY: St. Martin's Press.

Coleman, P. T. 2000. "Intractable Conflicts." In *The Handbook of Conflict Resolution: Theory and Practice*, eds. M. Deutsch and P. T. Coleman, 428-450. San Francisco, CA: Jossey-Bass Publishers.

Collier, P., and Hoeffler, A. 2002. "On the Incidence of Civil War in Africa." *Journal of Conflict Resolution* 46: 13-28.

Galtung, J. 1969. "Violence, Peace, and Peace Research." *Journal of Peace Research* 3: 167-191.

Gans, H. 1979. *Deciding What's News.* New York, NY: Pantheon.

Gitlin, T. 1980. *The Whole World is Watching.* Berkley, CA: University of California Press.

Hieber, L. 1998. "Media as Intervention: A Report from the Field." *Track Two* 7(4). http://ccrweb.ccr.uct.ac.za/two/7_4/p16_intervention.html Retrieved July 9, 2003.

Iyengar, S. 1991. *Is Anyone Responsible? How Television Frames Political Issues*. Chicago, IL: The University of Chicago Press.

Jacobson, T. L., and Jang, W. Y. 2002. "Media, War, Peace, and Global Civil Society." In *Handbook of International and Intercultural Communication 2nd edition*, eds. W. B. Gudykunst and B. Mody, 343-358. Thousand Oaks, CA: Sage Publications.

Jakobsen, P. V. 2000. "Focus on the CNN Effect Misses the Point: The Real Media Impact on Conflict Management is Invisible and Indirect." *Journal of Peace Research* 37: 131-143.

Livingston, S. 2000. "Media Coverage of the War: An Empirical Assessment." In *Kosovo and the Challenge of Humanitarian Intervention*, eds. A. Schnabel and R. Thakur, 360-384. Tokyo, Japan: The United Nations University.

Lugalambi, G. W. 2001. "The Role of Mass Communications in Preventing Conflict." In *A Continent Apart: Kosovo, Africa and Humanitarian Intervention*, ed. E. Sidiropoulos, 89-102. Johannesburg, South Africa: The South African Institute of International Affairs.

Lugalambi, G. W. 2003. "Media Freedom in Africa." In *South African Yearbook of International Affairs 2002/03*, 257-265. Johannesburg, South Africa: The South African Institute of International Affairs.

Makara, S. E., and Tukahebwa, G. B. 1996. "Politics, Constitutionalism and Electioneering in Uganda: An Introduction." In *Politics, Constitutionalism and Electioneering in Uganda: A Study of the 1994 Constituent Assembly Elections*, eds. S. Makara, G. B. Tukahebwa, and F. Byarugaba, 1-18. Kampala, Uganda: Makerere University Press.

Mamdani, M. 1995. *And Fire Does Not Always Beget Ash: Critical Reflections on the NRM*. Kampala, Uganda: Monitor Publications Ltd.

Manoff, R. 1998. "Role Plays': Potential Media Roles in Conflict Prevention and Management." *Track Two* 7(4). http://ccrweb.ccr.uct.ac.za/two/7_4/p11_roleplays.html Retrieved July 9, 2003.

Mittelman, J. H. 1975. *Ideology and Politics in Uganda: From Obote to Amin*. Ithaca, NY: Cornell University Press.

Nathan, L. 2000. "The Four Horsemen of the Apocalypse': The Structural Causes of Crisis and Violence in Africa." *Peace & Change* 25: 188-207.

Nnoli, O. 1998. "Ethnic Conflicts in Africa: A Comparative Analysis." In *Ethnic Conflicts in Africa*, ed. O. Nnoli, 1-25. Dakar, Senegal: CODESRIA.

Ocitti, J. 2000. *Political Evolution and Democratic Practice in Uganda 1952-1996*. Lewiston, NY: The Edwin Mellen Press.

Onadipe, A., and Lord, D. 1998. African Media and Conflict. London, UK: Conciliation Resources. http://www.c-r.org/pubs/occ_papers/af_media/acknowl.shtml Retrieved July 9, 2003.

Opotow, S. 2000. "Aggression and Violence." In *The Handbook of Conflict Resolution: Theory and Practice*, eds. M. Deutsch and P. T. Coleman, 403-427. San Francisco, CA: Jossey-Bass Publishers.

Robinson, P. 2000. "The Policy-Media Interaction Model: Measuring Media Power During Humanitarian Crisis." *Journal of Peace Research* 37: 613-633.

Tandon, Y. 2000. "Root Causes of Peacelessness and Approaches to Peace in Africa." *Peace & Change* 25: 166-187.

Tehranian, M. 2002. "Peace Journalism: Negotiating Global Media Ethics" *Harvard International Journal of Press/Politics* 7(2): 58-83.

Wolfsfeld, G. 1997. "Promoting Peace through the News Media: Some Initial Lessons from the Oslo Peace Process." *Harvard International Journal of Press/Politics* 2(4): 52-70.

7

What Role Should the Media Play in Conflict Transformation and Peace-building?

Stella M. Sabiiti

Introduction

The short paper presented here represents my thoughts, experiences and observations over a number of years in our country, in the region, on our continent and from observing the media unfold worldwide. I have shared these ideas several times in various settings, for I believe our work is not yet done until the media has accepted the fact that it indeed has a role to play in encouraging and enhancing peace-building, and until the rest of society acknowledges the fact that it will not achieve much without bringing the media on board.

Unless we widen and extend the contours of our understanding of what constitutes the media, we will fail to engage the entire media world in peace-building, because we will have failed to locate who exactly the media are. Briefly, these are what we refer to as *traditional* media: print (newspapers, magazines, etc.) and electronic (radio, television, video. etc,). But there is also the *alternative and creative* media comprising of theatre, drama, music, dance, poetry, *ebyevugo,* proverbs, sayings, etc.

The media is one of the most powerful forces we have. The media can create you or break you. The media is used to reach all corners of the globe, all villages, bedrooms, and the highest places of decision-making. It shapes our attitudes, helps us form opinions about important things in our lives and it influences our behaviour. Given all this power and influence, why then does the media not help in bringing about peace? Why can the media not come in and report positive stories during situations of conflict? Why does the media seem to be reporting only that which is violent, such as who is beating who in a battle, who is weaker of the two fighting forces, who has the mightiest weapons, who has killed more people, and not these islands of peace such as in Rwanda where some communities refused to pick up machetes and hack their neighbours to death. How about Hutus who hid their Tutsi neighbours? I find it most helpful to ask myself all these questions. The media has an immediate answer: peace does not sell! Here are some more reasons why the media does not play that positive role as the peace-builders would like it to.

Obstacles

1. The media is driven by the thirst to sell its product. Indeed, most media house owners are rarely journalists but shrewd business people.

2. A competitive paper, TV or radio station may fear being out-scooped by a rival media house.

3. A journalist works by deadline: There is therefore no time to hang around for the peace story to unfurl itself.

4. Hit it while it is still hot – some types of news are time-barred.

5. "Peace is soft news, in fact, it is not news at all," say the journalists.

6. Confrontation sells more than co-operation. This reflects the reality of the society.

7. Lack of or inadequate training of journalists.

8. Lack of financial resources to support the journalists.

9. Lack of adequate and appropriate equipment (tape recorders, radio sets, telephones, other studio hardware).

When can they play that positive role?

- Prevention is better than cure during peace time, as part of an early warning mechanism to advocate early action and response from all parties concerned.

- Supporting other players such as NGOs who are advocating conflict prevention.

- Being guardians of peace and harmony.

- In times of conflict, helping parties to a conflict crystallise the conflict in order to work on it positively.

- During the post-conflict reconstruction and rehabilitation, which includes forgiveness and reconciliation, not forgetting the role of traditional rituals for healing.

Experiences of Media Peace-building and Lessons Learned

CECORE's Intervention in Media and Peace-building

CECORE has designed a programme with the media in our region, with training workshops for the various elements of media, including community radio and women in the media. The main aim is to create confidence in the media so that it can become partners in peace-building. We achieve this by bringing together media actors with peace-building practitioners for cross-learning and moving forward together.

CECORE's Media and Peace-building Programme Strategy

Strategic Objective 1: Regional media practitioners better trained to report fairly and accurately on conflict issues and in promotion of development, human rights, democracy and peace.

- *Activity 1:* Develop field-test and produce a training manual for media practitioners based on lessons learned and best practices.

- *Activity 2:* Develop and conduct peace-building training workshops for media practitioners from the region to train leading journalists in preventive journalism techniques which are expected to lead to fair and accurate reporting that promotes peace.

Strategic Objective 2: Civil society actors and policy-makers in the region mobilised in the access to and effective use of the media for development and peace building.

Activity 1: Create an electronic communications network (ECN) to:

- bring together practitioners in the media with those in research, training, mediation and negotiation and institutions interested in peace-building so that they are more actively engaged in practical prevention, management and resolution of conflict in the region.

- act as a forum for the exchange of information, news, skills, methodologies and resources in relation to peace-building in the region.

- serve as an outreach facility to global partners, constituents and collaborators beyond the Greater Horn of Africa region.

Activity 2: Develop and publish a practical resource handbook and video on peace-building and media coverage of conflicts to:

- provide critical information on lessons learned to media practitioners and other interested groups including development bodies, policy-makers, and the business community.

- mobilise civil society and private sector actors and/or organizations and policy-makers in the access to and effective use of the media for development and peace-building.

These Strategy as greatly influenced CECORE's work with and through the media. The following are as examples:

Media and Peace-building – Perspective of Both Categories of Practitioners

In 2000 and 2001 CECORE brought together national, regional and international media practitioners and peace activists to discuss three main issues – African traditional mechanisms of preventing and dealing with conflict, including reconciliation; best practices of peace-building and the role of the media in peace-building. Also present were organisations that combine media and peace work.

A lot of lessons were learned from the series of events organised around the topic of media and peace-building. A few examples are provided below to illustrate the point further.

A Perspective of Media Practitioners Who Work in Partnership with CECORE

It is important that we understand the journalist's perspective.

i)   At one of the gatherings was veteran Africa media expert, Veronique Edwards, who works with the BBC in London. This is her perspective, derived from years of working in conflict situations:

*   The media should try to present the information as in politically accurate and objective a manner as possible.

*   They should present the arguments, have discussions and debates and present the parties involved in any conflict with an enabling environment to put their case across.

*   They should act as facilitators to check dictators, arrogant leaders and political elites that sometimes foment violence with impunity.

*   They should allow people to tell their story, and desist from inflating a story for the sake of selling their product.

*   They should use appropriate language.

ii) Another well-know veteran Africa media practitioners is Shaka Ssali, who has worked with the Voice of America for a number of years, mainly covering conflicts affecting Africa. Here is his perspective:

*   Depending on how the media is used and on the people it reports to, the media at times might not have any interest in what is going on, especially if one is to note that it is human beings who run the media, and they all have flaws.

*   In the ideal world, the media has its objectives, role and need to be professional but in reality this is not always the case. At times the media succeeds and at times it fails to measure up to its role and objectives.

*   A journalist is a messenger who ought to be looking at him or herself as a servant of the truth, and not a creator or master of the truth.

*   A journalist should see, filter, listen and later package his or her work in such a way that most of the information will target the right audience.

- The aim of the media is to be accurate, comprehensive and to furnish information with a background or context.

- News reporting on conflict is not as easy as it sounds. The media must learn from the people on the ground, the victims themselves, the government that makes decisions and the opponents involved in any conflict.

- It is essential that the media exercises humility, avoids being arrogant, because humility is the best way of knowing and getting information from people.

i) A Ugandan journalist turned-diplomat, Adonia Ayebare has worked at many levels of journalism, from the national, to the regional, to the international and then at the UN level. Most of the time he was covering active conflicts on the continent. With this wealth of experience, Ayebare is now an international diplomat, representing Uganda in crucial assignments for peace.

Experience of Covering Conflict Stories: A Ugandan Working with the UN Media

- Covering conflict is an extremely dangerous pastime.

- Realise that a journalist is a human being, and self-preservation assumes paramount importance.

- You must know the conflict, the actors involved and the basic factors of the conflict very well.

- Develop contacts with the people on both sides of the conflict, as well as others in the conflict area.

- Be aware that you are no longer dealing with ragtag rebels, but with rebels who are technologically sophisticated with access to satellites, mobile phones, and who even know how to manipulate information and broadcast their own information themselves.

- Avoid covering only one side to a conflict. Seek out all the players and their views.

- Be very innovative because in conflict situations the parties involved tend to cover up a lot.

- If you are not actively promoting peace, at least do not instigate or increase violent conflict because of your coverage. This is akin to Mary Robinson's Do No Harm principles.

Summary

In summary these are the characteristics of and prerequisites for a good media practitioner, according to CECORE findings. He/she should be/have:
  - impartial
  - objective
  - fairn
  - commited to a just cause
  - factual
  - creative
  - accurate
  - a good listener
  - a sense of timeliness of the story
  - a good communicator
  - confidential
  - accountable

After getting an insight into the world of a journalist, it is helpful to know the perspective of a peace-builder.

A Peace-builder's Perspective

A peace-builder's role should be to encourage peace and positive relationships. When mediating a conflict, these are the key considerations:

- Understanding the scope of the conflict.

- Skills of conflict analysis: source of the conflict, the different levels of a conflict, whether the conflict is on the surface, whether it is only symptomatic (looking at the demands and positions of the parties); at a deeper level, with an examination of the real root cause of conflict (interests and needs), the real driving force behind the conflict.

- Impact of the conflict, the players and their motives, roles and attitudes.

- Skills of transforming conflict: communication skills including active listening, negotiation skills, mediation skills, reconciliation.

- The ability to separate the people from the conflict so that you are hard on the conflict but soft on the people.

Ethics and characteristics of a mediator:
- Impartiality
- Taking risks (in a violent conflict situation)
- Patience
- Talking less (the process belongs to the parties, not to the mediator!)
- Not taking sides
- Asking a lot of questions
- Gathering information
- Integrity
- Confidentiality

What mediators are committed to:
- creating agreement between the parties
- facilitating the process effectively
- creating a win-win situation

Common Ground between the Media and Peace-building: Key Considerations

The Way Forward

From the above brief analysis of both the peace-builder (mediator) and journalist (media), common ground can be found – those things that the two have in common:
- Credibility
- Impartiality
- Risk-taking
- Gathering information
- Talking to all parties involved
- Confidentiality

Case Studies

Case Study 1: IMPACS

In its operational framework for media and peace-building, IMPACS has analysed the media worldwide and classified the media along a 5-stage continuum; itself clustered under three categories. This work was enriched by experiences of journalist and practitioners, including CECORE.

Traditional Journalism, Transitional and Transformational Media

Category 1: **Traditional Journalism**

1. **Stage One: Conventional Journalism** – Here journalism often emerges in post-conflict environments or after prolonged undemocratic governance, and lacks standards of professionalism and produces inaccurate, sensational or partisan reporting. In other cases, Stage One journalism can remain controlled by the state or special interests, and lacking enshrined freedom from interference, it reflects narrow views in its reporting which inflame tensions in the society.

2. **Stage Two: Responsive Journalism** consciously strives for the ideals of accuracy, balance and context and includes explanatory, investigative and well-informed analytical reporting. It operates editorially with relative independence from its owners and has mechanisms for its accountability to the public and for protection from intimidation. As in Stage One, the security of journalists is an important objective.

Category II: **Transitional Journalism**

3. **Stage Three: Sustained Peace Journalism** - the **transition** stage between conventional journalism and overt programming for peace, is sensitised to conflict resolution principles and consciously considers the consequences of its reporting on underlying causes of conflict

Category III: **Transformational Media**

4. **Stage Four: Intervention Media** is intentionally **pro-active** media-based intervention, beyond conventional journalism driven by commercial or competitive advantage. It is usually designed for a specific audience and purpose. It is often the product of an outside intervener such as an international peacekeeping force or an NGO and is often deployed in a conflict or post-conflict environment. It can be media intended to counter hate propaganda, or to provide immediately practical information such as election and voting practices, refugee reunification, education or health advice.

5. **Stage Five: Intended Outcome Media** is creative media intervention directly intent upon **reshaping attitudes**, promoting reconciliation and reducing conflict. It is not conventional journalism. The content is determined by its appropriateness to fostering peace. The programming and delivery mechanisms can be innovative adaptations of a popular culture such as radio and television soap operas and dramas, or street theatre and more. Media workers may play a role themselves as conciliators in the field.

Case Study 2: Search for Common Ground

Search for Common Ground is an international NGO founded in 1982 and based in Washington, DC. It works around the world in many aspects of conflict prevention, transformation and resolution. Search's strategy is fundamentally not to have only one approach but rather to be responsive without imposing any solutions or methodologies that the organisation brings. It has a toolbox of various approaches that have been tried and used in various countries in conflict, but these approaches can be adapted or modified to fit a particular situation. Search works with parties involved in conflict to enable them to solve their problems, speak together and to resolve their conflicts. They believe the media is a tool used to forward an agenda. Their agenda is to sell peace! They see the media as a problem-solving tool for parties in conflict and for encouraging and sustaining good relationships.

Search's models for conflict transformation

- Model based on community involvement: This is a process that promotes participation, interaction, and the development of mutual understanding using radio, video, or whatever technology available to communicate, in the hands of the community in question itself.

- Model capturing or model behaviour and modelling best practices: This model demonstrates practices that can be used by others. It is mostly used in documentation

- Responsive programming model: This is mostly used in places where the media has been used to foment hate, violence and stimulated killings. In such situations the media can be used to give voice to the people who are not polarisers.

- The curriculum-based programme model: This is the newest of media work that Search for Common Ground has been involved in outside Africa, such as in Yugoslavia, especially in Macedonia. It is a methodology that involves development of a very sophisticated curriculum for change in attitudes and behaviour, which then becomes applied by a production team. It is subject to intensive format research and evaluation, which feeds back into the programme.

In Africa Search for Common Ground operates studios with local media and peace experts in Liberia, Sierra Leone, Angola, Burundi, South Africa and the D.R. Congo.

Conclusion

Although many journalists still insist it is not their job to be involved in peace-building, the above examples clearly indicate the importance of the role the media can play as proactive actors, and the positive impact peace actors can create when they work hand in hand with the media, including creative, locally accessible media. The training manual and material CECORE has developed out of its experience working with and through the media will go a long way in promoting this interface.

Some useful websites

www.augie.edu/dept/coth
www.cecore.org
www.sfcg.org/cgpmain.htm
cross lines: www.ichr.org/xlines/xlinback.html
Fairness and accuracy reporting: www.fair.org
Headlines and soundbites: www.mediastuides.org/CTR/publications/hsb/index.html
Journalists at war: www.easynet.co.uk/LIRE/wars.htm
Media warfare: sunset.backbone.olemiss.edu
Media Studies Center: www.freedomforum.org/whoweare/media.asp
IMPACS: www.impacs.org

References

Mogekwu, Matt (2001) *Media and Peace-building: the Imperative for Re-orientation.*

Search for Common Ground videos.

IMPACS (2002) *An Operational Framework for Media and Peace-building.*

CECORE (2000) *The Role of Media in Peace-building*: *Experiences and Best Practices of Peace-builders and African Traditional Methods in Conflict Resolution, Reconciliation and Forgiveness.*

European Centre for Conflict Prevention/European Centre for Common Ground/IMPACS (2002) "The Power of the Media".

CNN Broadcasts.

BBC Broadcasts.

Discussion with journalists.

8

Behind *The Monitor's* October 10th Shutdown

David Ouma Balikowa

The shutdown of *The Monitor* newspaper on October 10, 2002 and the subsequent occupation of its offices for a week by state security agents, rekindled the debate about the state of freedom of expression, speech and the media in Uganda.

To a significant number of people, the closure and seizure of *The Monitor* came as a big surprise. The regime in power had created an almost believable impression that it had outgrown the often-too-easy temptation to resort to extreme measures when dealing with the media.

The seizure, which led to a one-week absence of the 11-year-old publication from the streets, succeeded in puncturing this myth. In doing so it reminded the world that the struggle for freedom of speech and the media was still an unfinished business in Uganda.

It was therefore not surprising that the public took to the FM airwaves with much zeal to debate the issue. A significant number of callers took turns to lambast government for over-reacting to *The Monitor's* story that an army helicopter had crashed while fighting the Lord's Resistance Army (LRA) rebels in northern Uganda. They argued that even if the story had been untrue, it did not warrant the invasion, seizure and shutdown of the publication and occupation of its offices by armed men.

The issues behind *The Monitor* closure are equally revealing. Besides exposing the government's bare-knuckled ill intentions against the critical independent media, it rendered bare the sad fact that the government had all along gravitated towards such extra-judicial actions. The legal hangovers from the colonial era, plus the unresolved political questions — which *The Monitor* shutdown reminded the world of — had always provided the government with both the reason and draconian apparatus to harass the media in an attempt to either control or silence it.

Similarly, the shutdown reiterated two critical things: first, that the media landscape in Uganda was — despite being liberalised – still far from being leveled; and secondly, that the struggle to rid it of landmines in the form of draconian/nefarious laws and extra-judicial sanctions in dealing with the media, must intensify if the media must discharge its democratic role.

Political Factors

The media is often the thermometer by which a country's political maturity is measured" (Tetty J.W. p16). It could also be said that in a democracy, a free media is the butter with which the democratic bread is eaten.

The analogies above describe the dialectic relationship between the media and the process of democracy. Much as the media has the role of shaping the political landscape as a means of bringing about democracy, the political landscape – as an end — to a large extent determines the level of media freedom and its sustainability.

An unlevelled political landscape often leads to tensions between the media and the state. The undemocratic regimes – slaves to wielding excessive power – in the process often rake the media landscape, leaving it bruised and unlevelled.

So while liberalisation of the media is perceived to be an indicator of media freedom and hence democracy, this assumption can be quite misleading in the context of political monopoly. The sustainability of a liberalised media and the supposed freedom of the media and speech as an outcome, are often undermined by the political monopoly – which in the Ugandan situation is epitomised by the Movement government. The Movement has monopolised the political space by maintaining a *de facto* ban on opposition political party activity for the last 17 years.

Whereas the current government has – in contrast to past regimes — permitted some level of media freedom, it is more often than not borne out of tactical interests than any conviction to win the approval of the donors who tend to equate freedom of speech and the media with democracy (Balikowa O. D. 1995).

If the independent media has tried to exist, it is not entirely because of the mere abstract declarations of principle by the Movement government to uphold a free media. The best measure can be found in the practice and adherence to such declarations.

To exist as a free press, the independent media, especially *The Monitor*, has constantly suffered the brunt of state harassment. There is hardly a year that passes without a member of its editorial staff being arrested, prosecuted or quizzed by the police or army.

Journalists have endlessly been banded together and branded enemies of the government. President Museveni hardly completes a public speech without equating the media, especially *The Monitor*, rebels or with supporters of terrorists.

Other indirect forms of censure such as advertising bans were applied against *The Monitor* between 1993 and 1997. If the government finally resorted to shutting down the publication in 2002, it is because it had tried all other forms of harassment without succeeding in cracking its critical independent stand or taming it.

The total effect of this puts government at odds with its declaration to uphold the principle of freedom of the media, speech and expression. Arguments can be made about the extent, but still that does not erase the critical question about the disconnect.

The fact that the closure of *The Monitor* came in the post-election period cannot be ignored either. The 2001 elections raised the stakes and the political landscape is likely to become even more uneven as we draw closer to 2006, the next election year.

It is, therefore, not a million dollar question as to why a government that had tried to exist uneasily along a critical and independent media, should finally succumb to the temptation of shutting down a newspaper? It simply demonstrated that the little freedom the media has enjoyed was on the whim of some individuals in government. The closure simply reminded Ugandan journalists and the world at large that the little freedom they had enjoyed is still built on clay ground, surrounded by shaky and fragile politics. In a nutshell, media freedom is still far from being institutionalised. A government that is a slave to resorting to extreme measures at the mere mention of political pluralism, is equally prone to unleashing all forms of censorship against the media at the slightest opportunity.

The sparks ignited by the post-election period will not stop with *The Monitor* closure. It might be just a herald of worse things to come. *The Monitor* closure coincided with strange but calculated happenings on the political scene. What began as isolated calls by some people to give

President Museveni another term beyond what the constitution permits him, is turning into a reality and has triggered sensational happenings across the political scene.

But neither was the closure of *The Monitor* the first strange post-polls event. The *bimeeza* (live outside political broadcasts) had already begun smelling bad to some people in government months back. The campaign to ban them shifted into high gear soon after *The Monitor* one-week shutdown.

A number of FM radio stations were also being compelled to stop broadcasting interviews with exiled politicians. Forget the fact that the government is often too quick to point to the many FM stations as the best measure of media pluralism and hence "its" tolerance of a critical media.

It would be stating a truism if one asked whether the government has been able to stop to ask why the closure of *The Monitor* attracted much more debate and attention worldwide than the story in dispute. Essentially because it recognises the fact that a free media has the potential to expose selfish designs and bring them to public scrutiny.

In one of the numerous debates of the closure, Prof. Fredrick Jjuko made a remarkable observation which provides valuable insights into how the government understands freedom of the media and how it wants it to operate.

He said that by liberalising the media, the government invited people to invest in it as a business, not necessarily to be a democratic channel of expression. That the government was happy with a media that does not produce ideas but delivers advertisers to audiences.

But it is turning out that the public wants ideas and not only adverts. Those who rushed to invest in the media were inevitably bound to run afoul of government over content – the "necessary evil in business" of this kind.

Is it then surprising that the first and perhaps only thought that the government came up with to "hurt" *The Monitor* was to close it?

In the process they even forgot that *The Monitor* was one of the few publications they were waving to remind the world of freedom of speech, media and democracy in Uganda. If that was an oversight, at least they can be excused for not having realised that in a country where the opposition is banned, the media is looked at as the only channel of free thought. The closure was bound to cause an uproar worldwide.

The above arguments lead to one basic conclusion: The closure of *The Monitor* on October 10 offered the best testimony that media freedom and a liberalised media can only flourish in a pluralistic political environment which Uganda is not yet. The Movement regime is effectively a one-party state, a fact that makes it allergic to free speech and a critical, independent media.

Where Does the Press Go from Here?

This is why in civilised societies, there is a willingness to tolerate a mistake by a newspaper because that is not in the least tradable with the wider value of a free media and society.

The critical issues arising out of *The Monitor* closure transcend the question of whether the story in dispute was true or not. It is not the denial of a story by the government that makes it untrue. Disputes of that nature are best resolved through courts of law. That is what the rule of law – and democracy — is all about.

In a democracy, errors committed in the exercise of free speech can only be tolerated. It is considered not too high a price to pay for the preservation of the wider principle and value of free speech, media and democratic society.

Resorting to punitive measures in case of errors can only be warranted by a demonstrable harm to the public interest. Even then, such actions should be within the democratically acceptable civil litigation context, not extra-judicial acts as was the case with *The Monitor* closure.

The German case of the weekly news magazine *Der Spiegel*, founded in 1947 by famous journalist Rudolf Augstein, provides the best reference for *The Monitor* closure.

The news magazine had a high reputation throughout Europe for its investigative reporting and exposure of abuse of office and scandals. In 1962, it exposed the financial problems of the German armed forces. The story suggested that despite the huge sums of taxpayers' money being spent on defence, the German army would be unable to fend off a communist attack.

In October 1962, 60 federal police raided *Der Siegal's* Hamburg offices, sealed and searched it and arrested three staff members. Augstein was also later arrested and detained on charges of treason.

The arrests sparked off worldwide protests. The German public took to the streets to protest the repressive action against the freedom of the media.

Shaken by public opinion, the defence minister Franz Joseph Strauss, who had been criticised in the magazine article, was forced to resign from cabinet in December 1962. He never held any cabinet position again and stood unsuccessfully for German chancellorship in 1980.

Augstein was released three months later and the charges filed against him dropped on May 14, 1965 after the accusations levelled against him were proved to be without foundation.

The *Der Spiegel* saga proves the point that the principle of freedom of speech and the media is far greater and should be upheld at the expense of tolerating errors. The German public protests proved the fact that extra-judicial interventions are more of a threat to a free democratic society than what the state often perceives as seditious or treasonable information.

From the above, the way forward for Uganda after *The Monitor* shutdown is crystal clear.

Prince Charles of Wales, while speaking at the 300th anniversary of UK's first newspaper, the *Daily Courant* at Fleet Street in March this year made what I consider a remarkable statement:

"From time to time you (the media) get things wrong – everyone does. But most of the time you are seeking to keep the public informed about developments in society, to scrutinise those who hold or seek positions of influence, to uncover wrongdoing at national level, in business or in local communities, to prick the propensity of the overbearing, and – a point often forgotten – to entertain us."

Two years ago, the state-owned *New Vision* ran a story that angered the army and the government. The paper reported that army officers were stealing cars, re-spraying them and selling them in the Democratic Republic of Congo.

The army issued a strong denial. But I suppose logic prevailed on government and the *New Vision* was not closed.

About three years ago, a plane carrying Col. Jet Mwebaze (RIP) crashed on its way to the Democratic Republic of Congo. *The Monitor* reported that Mwebaze, the pilot and other travellers had died in the crash.

The *New Vision* ran a story quoting then Minister of Defence, Steven Kavuma, saying that all the people on board that plane were alive. By the end of the day, it was quite clear the minister had given the *New Vision* wrong information.

The media did not ask the minister to resign because we all make mistakes. The army loses battles and the President often blames the failure to end the wars with rebels on the army's inefficiency. Junk equipment, undersize uniforms, and expired rations have in the past been bought. But even such costly errors are not enough excuse for the government to seize the army headquarters and close it for a week as it did with *The Monitor*.

Even as we strive to remind ourselves about the need to ensure accurate reporting among other standards, the way forward is restraint, especially on the part of the government.

Good institutions thrive on strict observance of the highest forms of professional standards. But no institution, be it government, parliament or even the judiciary can totally insulate itself from professional shortcomings. And when that occurs, the world should never be brought to an end.

But for the government to institutionalise restraint, it must rid our legal books of un-constitutional laws. The laws of sedition and publication of false news are colonial hangovers and should be scrapped from the books and instead the government should resort to civil litigation where the need arises.

The media too has to wake up and realise that not one among their number is safe if they are not united. The ban threat does not only hang over one media house. The newspapers and FM radio stations all face a common destiny.

Lastly, the government has to realise that media houses may belong to the owners who can be hurt by shutting them, but such moves hurt audiences in their millions too. It also portends a bleak future for media training institutions such as the Department of Mass Communication at Makerere University. If the media remains an endangered species, the journalism schools are equally doomed.

References

Tettey Wisdom J (2001) 'The Media and Democratisation in Africa: Contributions, Constraints and Concerns of the Private Press' *Media, Culture & Society* Volume 23 No. 1 p3-31.

Balikowa David O (1995) 'Media Marketing; an Essential Part of a Free Press in Africa' *Media, Culture & Society* Volume 17 No. 4 P604-613.

9

Partnering Civil Society with the Media in Peace-building

Deusdedit R.K. Nkurunziza

Introduction

The term "media" is very broad and refers to a number of issues. In this paper the term "media" is used to refer to news-media, the press, publishers, journalists and all those who constitute the communications industry and profession. Society today enjoys a good number of media channels, for example the television in the living room, the newspapers, the radio at home and in the car, the computer at work and the posters on the notice boards. All these are disseminating information which in turn has impact on civil society.

Civil society is one of those concepts that elude definition. For the purpose of this paper the concept of civil society is used to cover all those organisations that occupy the intermediate realm between the family and the state. The paper later discusses the foundations of civil society. Peace-building on the other hand is a dynamic ongoing process of interdependent actors, roles, functions and activities. Peace-building is an affirmation of civic freedom and a constitutive component of liberal democratic civic culture whose function is to produce the attitudes and dispositions required for a culture of peace. The media has the task of contributing towards the formation of a liberal democratic civic culture and promoting the autonomy and rights of the individual, thus laying the foundation for the culture of peace.

Partnering civil society and the media means that there is a dynamic link between the two.

The media without civil society is a product without a consumer, and civil society without the media would be like a body without life; it would mean an isolated and ultimately a dead civil society. The media is the nerve system of modern society.

139

To have life and dynamism in civil society, the media is necessary. Without the media, most people in civil society would know little about events happening beyond their immediate neighbourhood. The media not only vitalises civil society but also has a powerful impact on how people view the world. The media, even when it can be biased or limited, provides civil society with a picture of what is happening around the world. The media, therefore, is a powerful partner in peace-building; it informs civil society and civil society can in turn inform the media. While the media has so far capitalised on conflict, violence and war as top news, this paper argues that it is high time that the media also captured peace as hot news. Peaceful options such as mediation, negotiation and other collaborative problem-solving techniques should be covered by the media. In the course of peace initiatives these are not sufficiently reported by the media. Consequently they became invisible and as such are not often considered as possible options in the management of conflict. The media can be a stabilising and civilising force. In partnering civil society and the media, this paper urges the journalists to use the power of the media to build peace rather than report on conflict from a distance.

Foundations of Civil Society

The word "society" has its origin the Latin word "socius" in which means "fellow". In simple terms, therefore, society has to do with "fellowship" and relationship. Society implies a dynamic relationship for common good. There are different approaches to understanding society. For example, the traditional approach distinguishes between natural societies and voluntary societies. Natural societies include the family and civil society; while voluntary societies include a business co-operation, a school, a church or university. The family and civil society are the most basic and necessary societies for human activity and human development.

Hegel sees a relationship between the family, civil society and the state. The particular interests which are common to everyone fall within civil society and they lie outside the absolutely universal interest of the state proper.

Hegel defines civil society as – "an association of members as self-subsistent individuals in a universality which, because of their self-subsistence, is only abstract. Their association is brought about by their needs, is only abstract. Their association is brought about by their needs, by the legal system – the means to security of person and property – and by an external organisation for attaining their particular and common interests. The external state is brought back to and welded into unity in the constitution of the state which is the end and actuality of both the substantial universal order and the public life devoted thereto."

For Hegel, civil society is an abstract entity which only manifests itself and finds its concrete form in the constitution of the state. The sphere of civil society passes over into the state. The state is the actuality of the idea of civil society and manifests civil society. The state has immediate actuality in the constitution or constitutional law, international law and gives its actuality in the process of world-history. According to Hegel, therefore a state is an organised civil society, with government and laws (constitution) and international relations.

The government on the other hand is the agency of the people that ensures the internal order and cohesion of civil society. It has a governing and co-ordinating function to ensure harmony, unity and peace of all in civil society. The actual task of governing is the art of politics/political activity and those engaged in this public service constitute the "government". One can, therefore, understand the government as a functional organisation with the mandate of the people in service of the people and therefore in service of civil society. It is in this context that one can talk of the role of the media in civil society. In the Hegelian structure it means that one is focusing on the media and individual interests and rights as they may be represented and sometimes not necessarily represented and protected by the State and the Government. In other words there is an intrinsic conflictual relationship as one moves from the civil society, i.e. self-subsistent individuals and their spontaneous freedom to associate – to the state – which is the expression and manifestation of the concern and consent of all as expressed in the constitution. It is in this conflictual relationship embedded in the transitional political processes of the civil society –For instance, the process by which civil society through elections surrenders its authority to the state and the government and that is often called democratisation – that the media has a critical role to play by focusing on and highlighting the rights and interests of all stakeholders in the society.

Civil society is result of a freeself-organisation by individuals for their common good. The capacity and will to relate is intrinsic to human nature, consequently we speak of the social nature of man/woman. Man/woman relates freely to the other as part of his/her self-determination. Relating to others is part of our existential essence. In this sense, Marx is right when he states that the essence of man/woman is to be social. Aristotle also underlines this social nature of humanity when he says that every person feels naturally like a friend to the other persons. For Aristotle, the natural tendency of human beings towards is spontaneous friendliness; unfriendliness, tension, conflict and violence are afterthoughts, they are a result of circumstances and not something spontaneous. The human heart is soft and social by nature; for example, when one is in trouble, the immediate reaction is to help or cry for help-spontaneously.

People naturally tend to come together, form a society, and accept some form of leadership and authority. The ultimate goal of coming together is social cohesion for the good of everyone in society and not only for the majority. It is important to note here that the natural inclination of everyone in society is to be happy, as natural as flowers open towards the sun, or the sun rises every morning. This natural inclination to be happy and to love has an in-built conflict because it is actualised through a series of choices which constitute our experience of self-determination.

While the human person naturally tends towards the good, happiness and love, there is the freedom and the option to choose the opposite, either by accident or by intention. This is what I would call the metaphysical foundation of conflict within out own personal mode of existence. In other words, conflict is a perversion of the natural inclination; it is an ever-present negative inclination which causes unhappiness. It is a result of our actual choices and decisions. It starts on the level of decision, on the level of thought and ideas. This conflict, when not properly managed, spills over into the level of action. It starts within the individual and gradually spreads to his/her social relations and if not checked contaminates the whole community.

The state as an embodiment of civil society is supposed to pursue the welfare of its citizens. Ideally, the individual citizens should pursue the common good expressed in the state, but in practice the individuals work to pursue their own ends first. Hence the conflict between personal interests and the universal concerns of the community. This conflict can only be resolved through a process of education and conscientisation where the individual is liberated from the immediacy of personal desire to a more social vision through which his/her interests are ultimately realised. In this sense Hegal is right when he says:

... The final purpose of education: is liberation and the struggle for a higher liberation still; education is the absolute transition from an ethical substantiality which is immediate and natural to the one which is intellectual and so both infinitely subjective and lofty enough to have attained universality of form. In the individual subject, this liberation is the hard struggle against pure subjectivity of demeanour, against the immediacy of desire; against the empty subjectivity of feeling and the caprice of inclination. This disfavour showered on education is due in part to its being this hard struggle; but it is through this educational struggle that the subject will itself attain objectivity within, an objectivity in which alone it is for its part capable and worthy of being and actuality of the idea (Hegel, 1967).

The point I am trying to raise is the role of education in widening one's individual horizon from purely personal interests to national and global societal interest. Secondly, education is the means of attaining conflict management skills for peace-building processes. In this context the media has an indispensable role to play in educating civil society.

The family which is the need the civil depend on the goodwill and free activity of the individuals to work for the common good of all. This sounds idealistic, but it is the basic force of cohesion and the basis of the internal order of any society. Conflict arises in the social/political sphere when an individual or group of individuals feel sthat they are not getting their rightful share; when they feel either ignored, marginalised or exploited. Such a type of conflict disrupts unity and peace; once the conflict escalates to violence it injures the individuals involved and disintegrates society. In such context also the media has an indispensable role to play by presenting the information pertaining to the conflicting parties as politically accurate and as objective as possible.

The Role of the Media in a Democratic Society

The question of the role of the media in a democratic society is a complex one. On one hand there is civil society and on the other hand there is "media", and the two have to form a collaborative partnership. The issue I would like to raise here is that the media is not an abstract entity; the media does not operate in a vacuum; it is part and parcel of a concrete social-political-cultural environment. The media operates in the global environment of the civil society as a system; therefore the media should be seen as one of functional sub-systems of the civil society. In fact if we look at civil society. In this sense the media has been called "the culture industry" – while others have grouped the media with the family, the church and the education system under the heading of "ideological state apparatuses."

Civil society and the media can be conceptually separated but they are in reality intrinsically interrelated; they exert a mutual influence on each other. In the African sense, they are cousins to each other – independent but inter-related and dear to each other. It is therefore not only a question of partnering, but there is an indispensable vital dynamic relationship between civil society and the media. Without the media civil socity is dead and without civil society the media is lame. It is important here not to isolate the media from the social, political and cultural environment which produce it; but at the same time the media has to work for its own autonomy so as to achieve its own level of method and objectivity, advocacy, dissemination of knowledge and understanding of national issues. The media has an indispensable role in forming what is commonly known as the public conscience. In Uganda, for example, the media is practically the only medium available to civil society organisations to remain informed and to keep the civil society abreast of national issues. The media in Uganda has the task of creating the climate that facilitates the democratisation process.

The media is a means through which information is easily disseminated to civil society; the media keeps civil society informed. Today it is accepted that information is power, consequently the media empowers civil society. The media helps to create a well-informed civil society and facilitates free exchange of ideas and information among individuals of the same society. The media is a dynamic platform which helps the transformation of spiritual, social, cultural and political fanaticism by allowing the dissemination of a diversity of ideas and experiences, consequently creating an atmosphere conscious of plurality and diversity. The media helps to develop critical consciousness among the individuals in society. In this sense the media is cornerstone of a democratic society, where public debate and discussion are not only supported but are encouraged.

The Impact of Responsible Media on Civil Society

Having emphasised the role of the media in Uganda, one should go a step further and call for a responsible media, a media that practises professional ethics and cares about the people it covers. The media house and the individual editor or journalist are continuously standing before an ethical option either to be "constructive in approach or to be destructive", to be procative or conflictual. The current tendency of the media in Uganda is to be sensational, sometimes with a tendency to distort basic facts.

Responsible and reliable media is a prerequisite in Uganda for the empowerment of both the citizens and civil society organisations. A responsible media is a media that informs the public and serves the public interests, a media that is objectively acceptable and demonstrably justified in a free and democratic society. A responsible media cannot evade the question of "truth". The media in Uganda has to cultivate a culture of truth because "truth" ultimately has lasting value for individuals, economies and polities. Truth is the only emancipating and liberating factor of history. Consequently, the media has to aim at some level of objectivity so as to coherently influence the public conscience.

One has to note the fact that a considerable amount of our knowledge of others comes to us secondhand, through the media. The images the media uses provide us with benchmarks or points of reference. For example, for the majority of the Ugandans, the knowledge we have of President Bush is from the media; the image the media presents is the one which we cultivate in our minds. The media has that capacity to inform and to some extent influence our minds and actions.

It is the images, repeated and often dramatised, which constitue the major source of current information in society. There is a debate as to whether the media can change the attitudes and behaviour of people; if the media does not change people's attitudes, I think it is likely in the long run to modify and reinforce them. Definitely, the impact of the media is greater when all the media are saying more or less the same thing at the same time. If there is consistency, intensity and frequency, it becomes difficult for civil society to ignore the media's impact. Messages, images, viewpoints when repeated over and over again have an impact on our attitudes.

Because of its agenda-setting capacity, the media has influence upon the criteria which in the public domain decide what is important and what is not; what is normal and what is deviant; what is consensus and what is deissensus; what is significant or newsworthy and what is marginal. In fact the media has the capacity to form or manipulate the public conscience. Through the media negative influences can be as effective as positive influence.

One cannot underestimate the role played by the media in supporting, reinforcing and cementing patterns of social control and fashioning the symbols of legitimate government. It is at this level that some of us become very concerned when western agencies (such as BBC or Voice of America) report only the bad news from Africa; this creates a negative image and in the long run does harm to African integrity.

Positive Role of the Media

The media can play a positive reconciliatory role in moments of conflict and crises. A case in point is in March 2002 when the Army killed the Irish missionary priest in Karamoja at the hands of UPDF soldiers in March 2002. There was speculation in the press as to whether the Irish government would react by cutting off aid to Uganda; at the same time the press did present the clear position of the Irish consul that the incident would not lead to the cutting off of aid to Uganda because that would amount to punishing innocent people – recipients of this aid. In this case, the media tried to put pressure on the Uganda government and at the same time played an informative role, which maintained the good relationship between the two governments of Uganda and Ireland. Concerning the same incident the media was very critical of the hurried execution of the suspected culprits and raised questions and a debate about the death sentence. In my opinion, the media in Uganda handled this conflict in highly professional manner: keeping the civil society informed, raising the right issues and leaving questions open for public debate and room for individual judgement.

Another case which demonstrates the positive role of the media in moments of conflict is the conflictual crises in Muhabura Diocese. The media has kept the public informed; it kept the debate open through letters to the editor, through one could clearly hear both sides of the story. While the church bureaucracy was taking its time, diplomatically looking for an ecclesiastically acceptable solution, the press indirectly exerted some pressure by reporting on imminent violence. The story about stopping the Bishop-elect from entering the cathedral and some people being put in prison made the public think twice... One may say that the media coverage turned a local issue into a national one. I am trying to emphasise the positive role played by the media in the Muhabura conflict by keeping the public informed and by making a local issue into a national and global issue.

Incidentally, the media also indirectly put pressure on the Kisoro people to sort themselves out. The moment the media stops reporting a conflict its headlines, one gets the impression that the conflict is resolved while in reality the conflict might still be continuing.

Another example is the ethnic conflicts in Kibale district – it is to date a national issue and openly debated because of the media. The media has the capacity to identify local issues and to positively project them on to the public platform and raise both national and international concern. The media constitutes an indispensable nerve system of the global village.

The Negative Role of the Media

In her public lecture on "What role should the media play in conflict transformation and peace-building?" Stella Sabiiti (2001, p.9) speaks of "conventional journalism" which engages in inaccurate, sensational or partisan reporting. There are cases when the media can fuel crisis and conflict. For example, when one morning you read the headline of the *New Vision* saying "UPDF overcomes Kony" and the next morning you read the same paper with heading "Kony kills 65" etc, you wonder about the motive of the paper. In such circumstances one wonders whether the paper is reporting for purposes of passing on the information as it is or whether the paper is just looking for a sensational topic which will market it that day.

In certain situations, the media does play a negative role and civil society has to be attentive so as to get the media back into line through letters to the editor. The media is not absolute; it has a responsibility to civil society. So civil society also has a duty to keep the media on its toes.

The Provocative – Prophetic Role of the Media

The case which I would like to use to demonstrate the provocative and prophetic role of the media in civil society is the stories in the press concerning the conflict in Dr Kazibwe's family, the then vice president of Uganda. When Dr Kazibwe spoke about her experiences of domestic violence, some people felt the issue should not have come up in the press. It was as if the media was delving too deeply into the private life of the individual family. However, when you look at the issues the press was raising from the perspective of domestic violence, one discovers that the media was using a particular event to call public attention to a serious social phenomenon in our society. By reporting the individual case (which I think is not fair for the individual family) the media brought out clearly the extent, seriousness and gravity of domestic violence in Uganda. The media in this case was provocative and played its prophetic role; it is now up to the relevant organs of civil society to find a solution to a serious social problem that the media has brought to the attention of all concerned. The media played its provocative, indicative and prophetic role, but it cannot take decisions, which is the task of civil society. In the same vein the media has also tried to inform and to educate the public on the issues of child abuse and HIV/AIDS. In this regard the media stands out as watchdogs of the ethical constituency of civil society.

The Role of the Media in Peace-building

Traditionally, there are two schools of thought, the mass society tradition and the liberal pluralist schools of thought. The mass society tradition is for example who presented in Germany by Friedrich Nietzsche viewed the media pessimistically as constituting a threat to the integrity of the elite cultural values and the viability of the political institutions of democracy. He was concerned with the rise of mass culture – the social atomisation of "mass person". For example, Nietzsche thought that men were naturally divided between the weak and the strong; between those destined to be objects of the will of others and those who were self-willed; he therefore and constructed the social division between the elite and the masses as a product of the unequal distribution of such innate characteristics. The rise of the modern media threatened the bureaucracy of the elite. The mass society tradition criticised the media and the democratic forms of government as giving rise to the "tyranny of the majority". It called for constitutional reforms to curb and limit the power of the majority. The natural balance between the elites and the masses has been threatened by the advent of democracy, the development of the press and popular education.

The liberal-pluralist school of thought, unlike the mass society tradition, views the media as functioning and playing an important part in the democratic process and constituting a source of information that is independent of the government. I personally adopt the position of the liberal-pluralist school of thought and underline the role of the media in the peace-building process:

- Through the media, the government elites should be pressurised and reminded of their dependence on the majority opinion. While respecting the autonomy and the rights of the individual, the media should continually play a provocative, indicative and prophetic role to the civil society.

- The media should continually expose the elite who try to manipulate the "masses" through creating conflicts for their own selfish political ends.

- In conflictual situations, the media has a significant role to play by moderating influences that determine the extent to which the conflict is perceived or felt; the media can also influence how the parties approach the issue in the context of their wider relationships.

- The media provides a forum for conflicting parties to review their opinions and ideas; the media can, therefore, indirectly play a mediatory role thus bridging the gap between conflicting parties.

- The media can provide an atmosphere that is conducive to a win-win situation and this is a prerequisite for lasting peace. All parties involved must feel and know they have something to gain; such positive cross-cutting consciousness for a win-win solution can be influenced and attained by the media. This means that the journalists reporting in conflictual situations should focus not only on positions, but should also attempt to explore needs, interests, options and what lies underneath the positions being taken up by the conflicting parties.

- The media in civil society has also special task and role to be the voice of the voiceless. But it is civil society through its democratic procedures that will make concrete decisions and take actions which will ensure sustainable peace.

The Media for Peace-building Alternative Model

The traditional approach of "fighting frame" in news reporting seems not to be the best approach for peace-building because it tends to escalate a conflict rather than de-escalate it. The suggestion is for journalists to use the alternative model of "understanding frame". Instead of reporting focusing on positions, blaming parties in conflict, insisting on action and reaction, peace-building journalists would rather focus on issues, interest, options and solutions. The media should focus not only on the parties' position but also on why they take that position; not only on what should have been done, but also on what might be done in the future to resolve the problem; not only on a relationship gone sour, but on how to preserve and even build a better relationship in the future.

The challenge is for peace-building journalists to make a deliberate effort to separate the people from the problem. Peace-building reporters would also have to make use of non-inflammatory language, be balanced in the story-telling exercise and take into account human interests and analysis. One of the classical ideas in conflict resolution is to distinguish between the positions (that is the concrete demands) held by the parties and their underlying interests and needs. Interests are often easier to reconcile than positions, since there are usually several positions that might satisfy them. On the other hand, however, there is need to develop a critical capacity among media consumers. This would not only enable the media consumers to master their sources of information but also make them more demanding. The tendency today is for people to choose a media source not in order to look for objective authentic information but to support their own opinions and possibly even their prejudices. Peace-building media should not only look out for sensational stories, but also bring clear and objective analyses to a conflict situation.

Conclusion

The media is an integral part of any conflict situation – it is an actor like any other actor in conflict. As such the media must bear the consequences of its actions. The challenge, however, is that the media in conflict should aim at alleviating tension rather than exacerbate it. Understanding of the conflict by civil society organisations is generally shaped by the way in which information is presented by the media outlets. It is therefore important to recognise the impact that the media has on civil society organisations and to ensure that this influence is used appropriately. To a large extent, the opinion of the individuals in society about a particular conflict is greatly influenced by the type of media one has access to. The media, including television, newspapers and radio, greatly shape our worldview and perception of a particular conflict. It is therefore important for the individuals to be aware of the possible and inevitable bias of the media, hence the need to read and/or listen to as many different types of sources and accounts as possible so as to get a better picture of what is actually going on.

Civil society organisations on the other hand need to become deliberating, learning communities; and the media can help them by showing citizens how to see beyond the surface events and into the underlying causes of their problems. The media can set the agenda for civil society's informal discussions, at wedding feasts, beer parties and even at funerals. Through such discussions, the individuals in civil society organisations are helped to identify new possibilities for peace-building.

The media facilitates the process of making members of civil society into a learning community that is aware and conscious of problems and issues at hand, which enables them to form an opinion for personal decisions necessary to actively participate in sustainable peace-building processes.

Notes

[1] Concerning definition of the media, see, McQuail Denis, 2000 Mc Quail's Mass Communication Theory, London/New Delhi, Sage Publications pp.118-162; Paul Marns and Sue Thornham, 1996, Media Studies, A readers, New York University Press.

[2] Nkurunziza, R.K. Deusdedit, "The Role of Civil Society in Peace Building: The Case of Uganda" Nkurunziza R.K. Deusdedit & Mugumya Levis, 2003, Developing a Culture of Peace and Human Rights in Africa. African Peace Series, Volume One, Konrad-Adenaver-Stiftung, Kampala, p.23-33.

[3] Hegel, Philosophy of Right, Translated by T.M. Knox, Oxford University Press, London, 1976 p.110.

[4] Ibid, P.125.

[5] Harkheimer, M. and Adorno T.W. (1972) "The Culture Industry: Enlightenment as Mass Deception" in The Dialectic of Enlightenment.

[6] Althusser, L. (1971) "Ideology and Ideological State Approaches" in Lenin and Philosophy, and other Essays, London, Newleft Books.

References

Althusser, L. (1971) "Ideology and Ideological State Approaches" in *Lenin and Philosophy, and other Essays*. London: New Left Books.

Coser, L. (1956) *The functions of social conflict*, New York; Free Press.

Galtung, J. (1996) *Peace by Peaceful Means; Peace and Conflict, Development and Civilization*. London/New Delhi: International Peace Research Institute, Oslo, Sage Publications.

Hegel (1967) *Philosophy of Right* Translated with Notes by T.M. Knox. London, New York: Oxford University Press.

Deutsch, M., et al (1986) *Culture, Society and the Media.*London & New York: Routledge.

Horkheimer, M. and Adorno, T.W. (1972) "The Culture Industry: Enlightenment as Mass Deception" in the *Dialectic of Enlightenment.*

Howard S. Becker (1963) *Outsiders: Studies in the Sociobiology of Deviance,* US Free Press.

Lederach, J.P. (1996) *Preparing for Peace, Conflict Transformation across Cultures,*New York: Syracuse University Press.

Lederach, J. P. (1997) *Building Peace, Sustainable Reconciliation in Divided Societies,* Washington DC: United States Institute of Peace Press.

Sabiiti, S. (2001) "What Role Should the Media Play in Conflict Transformation and Peace-building?" Public Lecture, November, 5 Department of Mass Communication, Makerere University (unpublished).

Index

Acholi Religious Leaders Peace
Initiative (ARLPI), 62
African media, 45, 58; challenging
times for Conflict solutions, 45-61
African National Congress (ANC),
22, 23
Allied Democratic Forces (ADF)
(Uganda), vi, ix
Ant-intellectualism, 57
Armed conflicts in Uganda, vi, viii,
62-63, 79-81;
Background of, 68-72
Broadcast media, 2, 5, 7, 11, 12
Centre for the Study of Violence and
Reconciliation (SA), 26, 27, 39
Civil society:
and media , 144, 149; as a result
of a free self-organisation 141;
definition of, 139, 140;
foundations of, 140;
organisations in South Africa,
27; partenering – with media in
peace-building, 139-143, 150
CNN, 4, 5, 8, 9, 16, 109, 110, *see
also* Global news operations.
Communication, 63-64; and
information, 74, 88, 97, 98
Conflict and peace, 78
Conflict and peace, 78
Conflict resolution; *see also*
Diplomacy Its importance 1, 3, 6
Conflicts:
activists 115;
managing, 106-107;
practitioners, 115
Crimes, 22, 23, *see also* Criminality
Democratic Republic of Congo
(DRC), vi, ix, 48
Diplomacy, 2, 6;
definition of 2;
purpose of 2, 8;

tele, 1, 2-6
Electronic Communications Network
(ECN), 122-123
Front for National Salvation
(FRONASA) 68, 77
Gender discrimination in media
(Uganda), 52, 53, 54
Gulf War 1991, 5, 7, 8, 11
Human rights: approach to
development, 88;
as a right to communicate and
information, 96-99; biased
approach to information and
communication, 88, 89-90, 96;
Bill of Rights and Promotion of
Equality and Prevention of
Unfair Act 2000 (S.A) 34, 37;
Commission and the Media (in
SA), 33-38;
for Karimojong 100-101; Watch
(org.), 48.
Information, 72-73;
flow of, 10, 17, 72;
outlets, 6, 11, 12, 14;
source of, 11
International conflicts, 2
International human rights law, 92,
98;
international peace keeping forces
(S.A), 20
Judicial independence and rule of law
(SA), 20
Karamoja; *see also* Karimojong:
absence of law and order in, 92-
93;
cattle rustling and its impact in,
93, 94;
conflict and lack of
information, 88;
conflict development in, 93;
information and

communication in and about,
88; insecurity, possession and
misuse of guns, 91-92;
justice in, 93;
socio-economic, political and
cultural status of, 91;
state of communication, 95-100;
understanding – and
Karimojong 90-96.
Lord's Resistance Army (LRA), ix,
48, 73, 74, 79, 82, 132; effects of
– war, 79, 80, 81, 92, 104, 112
Lutwa, Okello (Gen.), 69, 71, 75, 77
Luwero Triangle, 73, 76
Journalism (ists)
as a profession, 26, 35;
objective –, 23, 29, 30, 124;
peace –, 23, 24, 25, 26, 35, 41;
responsive – 128;
traditional, 128;
transitional –, 128, 144
Media:
and armed conflicts in Africa,
viii, 6; and conflict
transformation, 120;
and diplomacy, 1, 4, 17;
and peace-building, vii, 17, 103,
115, 120, 123, 148-150;
and racism in SA, 31, 33, 43;
as a communication channel, 4, 5;
as a political thermometer –
133; characteristics of a good –
practioner, 126;
experiences of – peace-building
and lessons learned (Uganda),
122-125;
imperialism, 46;
influence on policies, 3-4;
in perspective, 108-109;
intended outcome, 129;
intervention, 128;
liberalisation of, 135;
marginalisation of peace by,
112-114;

negative role of – in Uganda, 147;
outlets, 5;
political culture of violence, 105;
positive role of – in Uganda,
146-147;
practioners, 13, 62, 123, 124;
prophetic role of, 147;
relation between military and, 1,
4, 5, 6, 17;
role of, 130;
role of the – in a democratic
society, 143-144;
sensitivity to – in Uganda, 110-
112;
social mandate of, 114-116;
transformational –, 128-130;
understanding of, 109-110
Museveni, Yoweri, 74, 77, 79
NRA (National Resistance Army),
69, 70, 71, 72, 82. *See also*
UPDF, struggle, 76
Obote, Apollo Milton (Dr), 69, 74,
75, 77
Pacification in northern Uganda, 73
'Peep show', 46, *see* Big Brother
Africa, 47, 58, 59
Pike, William, 73
Rwanda genocide 1994, viii –, Siera
Leone, viii
South African Law Commission, 38
Sudan People's Liberation Army
(SPLA), 67, 68
Tele-diplomacy, *see also* diplomacy
by way of television, 2, 3, 4, 9-
10, 11, 12, 15, 18
Television:
and diplomacy, 1;
as a mass medium, 45;
as a propaganda tool, 8-9;
as a quasi diplomat, 3; *see also*
tele-diplomacy;
as a source of information, 6;
challenges involving the role of

– in conflict resolution, 6-13;
developments in – technology,
3, 13; functions of, 3;
role and power of, 5-6;
roles of – international conflict
resolutions, 1-9
Truth and Reconciliation
Commission, 23, 35; and media
(in SA), 29-33, 43
UNLA (Uganda National Liberation
Army), 69, 71
Violence:
apartheid-related in SA, 26, 29;
as a way of dealing with conflict,
105;
complexity and inexplicability of,
38;
crime-related, 27, 28;
cultural –, 25, 105;
differences in –, 105;
in South Africa, 20, 23, 27;
irrational – against African
migrants in South Africa, 21;
political – in South Africa, 22,
27, 28, 29, 35;
related journalism, 22;
ridden society, 25;
structural – 105, 107
Visual media, 46
West Nile Bank Front (WNBF), 68

www.ingramcontent.com/pod-product-compliance
Lightning Source LLC
Chambersburg PA
CBHW021829020426
42334CB00014B/549